POLINA BARSKOVA

AIR RAID

Translated from Russian by Valzhyna Mort

Eastern European Poets Series
Ugly Duckling Presse
Brooklyn, NY

Air Raid
Copyright © Polina Barskova, 2021
Translation copyright © Valzhyna Mort, 2021
Afterword copyright © Polina Barskova & Valzhyna Mort, 2021

Eastern European Poets Series #47
Series Editor: Matvei Yankelevich

ISBN 978-1-946433-70-1
First Edition, First Printing, 2021

Ugly Duckling Presse
The Old American Can Factory
232 Third Street, #E-303
Brooklyn, NY 11215
uglyducklingpresse.org

Distributed by SPD/Small Press Distribution and by Inpress Books (UK)

Cover Art by Vladimir Zimakov
Typesetting by Raphael Schnee and Don't Look Now!
The type is Skolar PE designed by David Březina for Rosetta
Covers printed offset at Hodins Engraving
Books printed offset and bound at McNaughton & Gunn

The translation and publication of this book were made possible, in part, by grants
from the National Endowment for the Arts and the New York State Council on the
Arts, with the support of Governor Andrew M. Cuomo and the New York State
Legislature. This project is supported by the Robert Rauschenberg Foundation.

TABLE OF CONTENTS

9   A Sunny Morning in the Square

13   Auschwitz-Birkenau, a Guided Tour for American Students

17   Children's Literature

19   "After the war he found himself in the West"

23   Air Raid

33   Dachshunds

37   Encounter

41   A Guide to Leningrad Writers, Veterans 1941–1945

57   Joy

59   A Passionate Damsel, or the Exploits of Zinaida C.

71   Hampshire College Archive. Personae.

81   The Fish

85   Mercy

89   The Public Library in San Francisco

91   Mutabor

99   Romantic Walks Through City Cemeteries

111 Family Flight to Egypt

115 Ivan Turgenev to Pauline Viardot, A Letter

121 Catullus 68a Lisbon

125 Pottery/Poetry

131 International Day Of Sirens:
     A Conversation in Lieu of an Afterword

148 Notes to the Poems

AIR RAID

СОЛНЕЧНОЕ УТРО НА ПЛОЩАДИ

Т.П.

Еще вчера мое сырое тело
Взрывалось волновалось и хотело
Теперь оно как листик как листок
На поезде спешит на Белосток

Там сорок первый (Иль тридцать девятый?)
Там страхом все обложены как ватой
В коробке новогодние шары
Там живы все еще еще жары

Все обсуждают раннее явленье
И на столбу читают объявленье

«Явиться всем на площадь в шесть часов,
С собой иметь двенадцать штук часов,
С собой иметь двенадцать гончих псов,
С собой иметь заслонку и засов»

Все в городе молчат и говорят
На площади встречает их солдат
Во лбу сияет свастика горит
Во рту звезда и он не говорит

«Куда девать нам псов, засов, часы?
Колени наши влажны от росы
Горящих листьев полны наши рты
Зачем мы здесь солдат с тобой на ты?»

A SUNNY MORNING IN THE SQUARE

to T.P.

My half-baked flesh
stuffed with its own tricks
finds itself as a leaf
or a leaflet caught in the rush
of a train to Białystok.

Białystok stuck in 1941 (1939?).
Białystok padded in fright like a Christmas star
stored away in its box.
People still wake there
alive   living   ablaze.

They discuss an earlier event
and read an announcement:

"You are to appear in person on the square at six,
bring only your wrist watches, in the amount of twelve,
bring only your greyhounds, in the amount of twelve,
bring only one bolt and one hatch."

Białystok grows silent and speaks
stocked with soldiers in the amount of one,
between his brows a swastika shines,
in his mouth a star shuns speech.

"Where should we shovel our hounds, our watches, our hatch?
Our knees bleed dew,
our teeth rake burning leaves,
why, shiny soldier, are we so sweet with you?

Солдат внушает им: здесь будет цирк
Вам чудеса предложит наш царек
Солдат вальяжно им: ох, будет крик
Historia навяжет вам урок

Прощенья/превращенья в семь часов
Раздастся лай и грохот гончих псов,
Уже к восьми свобода и отбой,
Когда умрешь, скажи. И я с тобой.

The soldier curses at them: we'll build a circus!
Our circus king will show you his tricks.
A star built of smoke and scream!
History crams a lesson down your throat.

Mercy me/Master me on the square at seven,
greyhounds bark, hatches shine, wristwatches bang,
by eight the square is ready for bedtime
and you crack like a glass Christmas star. Arrr arrr

ОСВЕНЦИМ, ЭКСКУРСИЯ ДЛЯ АМЕРИКАНСКИХ СТУДЕНТОВ

I

Подъезжая на микроавтобусе под польскую деревеньку О.
Удивляю себя—чего это, я не чувствую ничего.

Вроде душа моя развороченная бесчувственная десна,
Развлеченье дантиста, роденбаховский город сна.
Главное двигаться словно вода в канале—то есть не двигаться.
Лишь шевельнёшь рукой
—сумасшедшие тени вмешаются в твой покой.

Все эти Розы, Людвиги, пронумерованные для нас,
Чтобы мы их пересчитывали, пока поступает газ.

Пересчитывали впрочем косвенно: горшки, протезы, очки,
С красной каёмочкой, с чёрной каёмочкой волшебные
    башмачки,

Чемоданы, волосики, пепел, провисшие облака,
Студентки фиолетовая от холода рука
Впивается в зонтик. Кукушка
В Биркенау—скажи, сколько лет ещё
Мне навещать нравоучительные бараки?
Холодно холодно горячо:
Жмурки цивилизованного сознания.

Ничего не чувствую кроме стыда
Сбрасывать пепел Marlboro
На пепел, произведённый здесь, пролитый сюда.

AUSCHWITZ-BIRKENAU, A GUIDED TOUR FOR AMERICAN STUDENTS

I

When the minibus nears the Polish village of Ausch.,
I feel numb. My pneuma, a
                    cut open gum,
a game for a dentist, Rodenbach's drowsy Bruges.
Focus on moving the way water in channels moves—which
        it doesn't. I stir—
and mad shadows disrupt my numbness.

All these Roses, Ludwigs, thoughtfully numbered for us,
to count, to recount through the gas.

The recount was roundabout: bowls, prosthetics, red-
framed glasses, fairy slippers laced black,

suitcases, hairs, ashes, sagging skies,
a hand of a female student purple from cold
clutches an umbrella. A cuckoo
of Birkenau, how many years more
will I visit educational barracks?
Cold, cold, cold, hot:
hide-and-seek of the civilized consciousness.

I am numb except for the shame
of brushing Marlboro ashes
on the ashes made here, shed here.

II

Вот этот камушек есть памятник ему.
Вот это облако окурок лютик пёс—
Всё, что с собой он взять не мог во тьму,
Хоть до последнего не жаловался нёс.

Вот это дерево сортир скамейка мак—
Весь мусор ужаса, отчаянья дерьмо,
Я, расфуфыренный, самодовольный маг,
Несу тебе—валяй, смотри кино

Вещей, которые резвятся, как во сне:
Подмигивает смятое пенсне,
Кастрюлька хрюкает, будильник правит ночь,
Корябает огрызок-карандаш:
Владелец наш, кормилец наш, поилец наш,
Тебе и рады бы помочь
—не знаем как.
Вот этот камушек тебя последний знак.
Не-восклицательный. Заноза. Зонтик. Злак.

II

This pebble here is a monument to someone.
So is a cloud a stub a poppy a dog—
Whatever no one can carry into the night,
carrying it, no one complained.

This tree here WC buttercup bench—
the garbage of horror, despair's filth,
vain, adorned, and duende'd, I
carry to You—watch this film

of things, whirling as in a dream:
a battered pince-nez winks,
a cooking pot snorts like a pig, an alarm clock squares the night,
a gnawed pencil scrapes:
Our Master, daily feeder and quencher,
here we are, glad to help—
but how?
This pebble here is the last sign of you.
A point. Of no exclamation. Splinter. Spike. Grain.

КНИЖКИ С КАРТИНКАМИ

Они пытали их обоих.
Какого цвета на обоях
Они оставили следы?
Конечно только золотые,
Конечно только голубые,
Горения слюны слюды.
Смотри ж на дивные оттенки:
Они остались на застенки,
Сюда идём мы как в музей.
Что видим мы в музее этом?
Вот видим: стрекозиным летом
Блуждает череда друзей,
Хармс сторонится Шварц хохочет,
Олейников его не хочет,
Знать, он лежать у речки хочет
И жабу палочкой крушить.
Их путь ещё не кончен, — начат,
И все они уже да значат
Поэзию и крутят нить.
Сквозь стрекозу, сквозь паутину,
Смотрю на жаркую картину
И вижу их живыми не.
Один во льду, другой на дыбе,
Введенский плавает на рыбе,
Мерцает Вагинов на дне.

CHILDREN'S LITERATURE

Both were tortured.
What color traces
did they leave on the wallpaper?
I bet you golden
I bet you blue
Burns of crystal, drool.
Observe droll colors
preserved in the confines.
We come here to a museum.
What do we see in this museum?
We see: a trail of fellows
who dragonfly on summer days.
Kharms shies away Shvartz ha-has
to Shvartz Oleinikov prefers
to slug by a stream
poking a toad to death.
Their journey has just begun,
not ended, they stand
for poetry and weave their thread.
Through web, through a dragonfly's wing,
I watch a blistering scene
and see them living not:
One in the ice, another on the rack,
poet Vvedensky floats atop a pike,
poet Vaginov twinkles on the river's bed.

«ПОСЛЕ ВОЙНЫ ОКАЗАЛСЯ
НА ЗАПАДЕ»

Старуха Гиппиус с просторным кадыком
Глядит с нечистого балкона
Как офицер играется с щенком.

Она глядит завороженно
Как форма серая
Как говорил Верлэн
Как роза серая
Мерцает и тревожит
И выпускает хрящевидный стон
Сказать же ничего не может
Своим чудовищным безжалостным умом
Она поцокала и все сошлось в задаче
И рядом с ней тяжелоокий гном
Кивнул: не будет быть иначе—

Коль ту страну (не называй вотще)
Пожрало простодушье ада,
То, кто бы ни пришел
С мечом иль на мече,
Вот тот и станет нам услада.

Пусть для него позвякают слова
Как челюсти вставные наши.
И нищая седая голова.
И слава старая пусть наполняет чаши.

«Эх вы Иуды, ебаные в рот:
Век подотрет за вами это.
Как документы—тени жжет и рвет
Парижское беспамятное лето

"AFTER THE WAR HE FOUND HIMSELF IN THE WEST"

Old Lady Gippius,
of a tumorous Adam's apple,
from an unclean balcony
watches
an officer play with a puppy.

She is staring, bewitched,
at his gray uniform
or, as Verlaine would have it,
a gray rose in Paris
that sparkles and alarms.
Incapable of speech,
she lets out a cartilaginous moan.
Her monstrous merciless gray matter
heaves and finds a solution.
Next to her, a gnome carrying its eyelids' burden
nods: it wouldn't come to be otherwise

If that land (don't name it in vain)
descends into simple-souled
hell, whoever arrives
with a sword or—atop a sword—
he would be swell.

For him, let our words
clank like dentures.
For him, this bankrupt gray head.
For him, raised glasses of gone sparkling glory.

"You, Judas of a gagged mouth hole:
this century will wipe up the mess you left.
A summer—oblivious, Parisian—rips and burns

И жесты скверные
ужасных стариков
По-воровски поспешно спрячем
И самый смысл переиначим
их совершенно невозможных слов»

Геополитика! Тевтоны у границ!
Огонь и наважденья рейха!
Старуха Гиппиус брезгливых кормит птиц
Под ней шатается скамейка
А на скамейке, сбоку от нее
Все, кто ушел по льду, по илу
В самопроклятие, в безвидное житье—
В по-смертия воздушную могилу.
Кого блокада и голодомор
Вскормили чистым трупным ядом,
Кто, убежав НКВДшных нор
Исполнил заданное на дом:

Избыть свой дом, не оставлять следов,
Переменить лицо-привычку,
Среди послевоенных городов
В анкете ставить жирный прочерк/птичку
Приманивать: мы ниоткуда, мы
Никто, мы—выбравшие плохо.
Мы двоечники в строгой школе тьмы,
И чистоплюйская эпоха
Нас подотрет как пыль—до одного,
Чтоб следующим не было повадно
Рассматривать и плакать существо,
Чумные на котором пятна.

shadows like documents.
Creepy old immigrants
are making crude gestures.
Thief-swift, let us hide and alter
the very meaning of their impossible words."

Geopolitics! Teutons at the border!
Fire and infestations of Reich!
Old Gippius feeds the picky birds.
Under her, the bench creaks.
Next to her, on the bench, they
who have gone
over ooze, over ice
into self-damnation,
into eternal hiding.
They, nursed by the pure
corpse milk
of the Siege, of Holodomor,
who, having escaped the NKVD dens,
completed their homework:

Shed your home, leave no trace,
adopt new facial habits
in the post-war cities
mark the questionnaire
with fat crumbs of NOs/baiting
the birds from a safe distance:
we are from nowhere, we are
nobody, we made but one mistake,
failed students in the unforgiving school of darkness.
Watch this clean-freak of an epoch
wipe us up like dust, to the last speck of us,
a lesson to others not to look in tears at a creature,
plagued, pockmarked.

ВОЗДУШНАЯ ТРЕВОГА

Эти стихи описывают след, оставленный во мне чтением писем

Ну
Кому письмо пляши пляши
Кому письмо дыши дыши
Кому письмо пиши пиши

Штемпель:
«Возвращено» «вращено» враще
«Выбыл» был был был был был был был был был был былвы
«Доставить невозможно»
НЕ

ОТКРОВЕННО ГОВОРЯ МЕНЯ БЕСПОКОИТ ТВОЕ МОЛЧАНИЕ

Уже 10 часов
Уже 10 лет
Уже <пропущено> лет твое молчание тревожит меня

1. ТАТОЧКА ПИШЕТ ТЕБЕ ТВОЙ ПАПОЧКА

Ты на сердце моем латочка, ласточка.
Какой день сегодня? День — сегодня.
Здесь
каждый день сегодня.
Вчера нет завтра.

Помещаюсь я сейчас с одним военным
Помещаемся на одном отделении нар
Он внизу я наверху
Человек он неплохой
Каждую ночь он кричит на непонятном языке
Сначала я удивлялся, пытался хоть угадать языковую группу.

AIR RAID

These poems describe the trace left in me by the reading of letters

Erm
Up up jump who got mail
Down calm breathe who got mail
Write write write who got mail

Postmark:
"returned mail" "urn mail"   urrrrrrrrr
"doesn't reside at this address" doesn't doesn't this
"unable to deliver"
DE

FRANKLY SPEAKING I'M WORRIED ABOUT YOUR SILENCE

Already 10 hours
Already 10 years
Already <left out> years your silence worries me

1. TATOCHKA, THIS IS YOUR PAPOCHKA WRITING.

You are—on my heart—a patch, a pooch.
Which day is it today? Day's today.
Here
every day is today.
No yesterday tomorrow.

I am housed with one officer
We are housed on one bunk
He below me above
He is not bad.
Every night he screams in an unknown tongue.
At first I was intrigued, tried to guess the language family.

Теперь я грущу, томлюсь.
Ночью мне кажется, что это секретное сообщенье, если бы я
    смог его разгадать, я бы узнал,
когда увидимся мы с тобой.

Деточка!
Что сказать тебе еще?
Лечу свои зубы.
Скоро мне будут делать железные из нержавеющей стали,
так что скоро буду со стальными зубами, смогу грызть железо.
А как у тебя обстоят дела с зубами? Береги их детка, не запускай.

Октябрь 1941

2. МАЛЕНЬКАЯ ТАТА!

Это—я, твоя бабушка Большая Тата.
Бабушка бабочка бабушка бочка
Помнишь как на варикозных своих колоннах
Семенила Я за Тобой вдоль сада
Как ты стеснялась смеялась меня
Притворялась что ты сама по себе
Вот теперь ты и вправду сама
И я сама
в Саду.

Папа твой заболел и уехал недавно

Люди перезванивались и спрашивали: «Как ваше здоровье?»
И только слышали, тот заболел, та в больнице.
Все понимали, что это значит.

Now I languish, sad.
At night I wonder whether it's a secret message to me, if only I could
 decipher it, I would know
when I'll get to see you again.

Childkins!
What else?
I'm treating my teeth.
Soon I'll get iron teeth, stainless steel teeth,
so yes, soon I'll have steel teeth and will chew on iron.
How are your teeth? Take good care of them, sweet dove.

October 1941

2. LITTLE TATA!

It's me, your grandmother Big Tata.
Grandmother—grasshopper—grandbarrell.
Remember on my varicose columns
I trotted after you through the garden?
How you were embarrassed and mocked me,
pretended to be out by yourself.
Now you are indeed by yourself.
And me too
in the garden
by myself.

Your father grew unwell and left the other day.

People phoned each other: "How's your health?"
One was "unwell," the other "hospitalized."
Everybody knew what that meant.

Папа твой заболел и уехал недавно
А раньше когда он еще не уехал
Мы втроем ходили сюда к жолудям

Октябрь 1941

3. ЕДИНСТВЕННОЕ СОХРАНИВШЕЕСЯ ПИСЬМО ДЕВОЧКИ ТАТЫ, НЕОТПРАВЛЕННОЕ

Милый любимый Пунешенька!
Я их спрашиваю где я: это село Емуртла
Я их спрашиваю кто я: ты выковыренная
Откуда? Не отвечают, отворачиваются.

Я их спрашиваю что есть у меня?
Старое бабушкино платье и карандаш
Ботинок и мыла и конвертов нет.

4. «МНЕ УЖЕ ЖАЛЬ ВАС»

Карандаш; красными чернилами поверх текста письма
наискосок на первой странице: «т[оварищ]у Миллер И. Не
пишите, пожалуйста, на этот адрес письма на з.к. заключенного.
Его уже НЕТ. Мне уже жаль вас, что вы пишите ему письма
часто, а его нет. Пишу его новый адрес: Свердловская область.
Поселок Табары. 239/3.
[7 строк зчрк]
В конце просматриваются три буквы
иты
Повторять, пока не поймешь замысел писавшего
Повторять, пока не поймешь намерение цензора
причастие страдательного прошедшего времени
    множественного числа? Существительное? Прилагательное?
Вместе или раздельно?
Раздельно и вместе.

Your father grew unwell and left the other day.
But before he left
the three of us would come here, among acorns.

October 1941

3. THE ONLY REMAINING LETTER BY GIRL TATA, UNSENT

Dear beloved Sweetpoochkins!
I've asked them where am I: village of Yermurtla.
I've asked them who am I: dug
out of where? They turn away, say nothing.

I've asked them what do I have?
Grandma's old dress and a pencil.
Of boots, of soap, of envelopes, I have none.

4. "BY NOW I FEEL SORRY FOR YOU"

Pencil; red ink over the text of the letter, diagonally, on the first page:
"to c[omrade] Miller. Please stop writing letters to this address. He is
NOT here. By now I feel sorry for you writing to him so often while
he isn't here. I'm enclosing his new address: Sverdlovsk region.
village of Tabary. 239/3.
[7 crossed out lines]
At the end three letters could be distinguished:
led
Repeat this until you understand the sender's intent.
Repeat this until you understand the censor's intent.
Past passive participle, plural or singular?
A verb? A noun?
Spelled in one word or separately?
In one and separately.

5. ПРОСЬБА О ПОСЫЛКЕ

Заранее спасибо тебе родная моя за посылку о только бы
    она пришла!
Если можешь: бумаги и конвертов
Не отрывая от себя!
Не в ущерб себе!
Если ты можешь: самых дешевых продуктов
Не отказался бы и от собачьего жира
Так что если будут такие возможности у тебя, организуйте
    этот жир, посолив, чтоб не портилось, а при возможности
    немного подкоптив,
пойдет очень хорошо, только условно будем называть
    жир козьим.
Может быть когда-нибудь встретимся и я смогу быть
    благодарным тебе
и за хорошее отношение и за поимку собак.
Но если это не выйдет,
был бы рад отрубям
и подсолнечной жмыхе от масла либо
соевой либо хлопковой.

6.

Милая девочка!
Как меня радует что ты пишешь о себе писать нечего
Ленинградская жизнь вообще не подлежит описанию
Я страдаю модной болезнью (поносом) и хожу теперь с палкой
Но как меня радует, что ты пишешь
Папа твой он не пишет мы не слышали от него ничего давно
Моих писем он очевидно не получает совершенно
Посылала ему за это время денег два раза ответа
    положительно никакого
Так что мы даже предполагали что его там вообще не существует
И решили положиться на время

5. REQUEST FOR A CARE PACKAGE

Thank you so much in advance for the package oh please let it arrive!
If you can: send paper and envelopes.
But I beg you, only as long as it's not a sacrifice!
Not at the expense of your own wellbeing!
Send if you can: food, whatever is cheapest,
I won't turn down dog fat.
So if an opportunity arises, please organize the sending of this fat,
salt it so it doesn't go bad, if there's an opportunity to smoke it a little
that would be nice, but let's agree to call it goat fat.
Perhaps one day we'll see each other again, a chance to thank you
for your kindness and for the catching of the dogs.
If this doesn't work out
I'd be happy with bran
and oil meal or
soy or cottonseed.

6.

Darling girlkins!
How happy I am that you are writing—about me I have nothing to write.
Life in Leningrad defies description.
I'm suffering from a trendy illness (diarrhea) and walk with a stick.
But what happiness that you are writing.
Your papa isn't—we haven't heard from him in a long time.
It appears he has not been receiving my letters.
I've sent money twice,
                    got positively no response,
so it's safe to conclude that he isn't there.
We are relying on time now.

Я сижу в бомбоубежище, моя милая девочка
В темноте Я вспоминаю твое лицо
Эта радость от твоих писем
Бесконечно довольна, что тебя нет с нами
Все время вспоминаю тебя
Радость радость какая радость
три твоих письма одно за другим!
Как хорошо, что ты теперь не рядом со мной

7. P.S.

С сегодняшнего дня остается двенадцать месяцев и восемь дней
Ждать встречи с тобой любимая дочурочка доченька
....
С сегодняшнего дня остается десять лет
Меня судили и дали еще десять лет милая девочка
Старый срок, который я уже отбыл, не в счет
На этом кончаю письмо, так как кончается бумага и
    коптилка гаснет.

Скорей бы прижаться друг к другу
Не отрывая от себя.
«Когда вошли в квартиру, она была даже неразграбленная,
Но бабушка полусумасшедшая и полуживая».
Девочка: не отрывая от себя.

I'm sitting in a bomb shelter, my darling dove.
In the dark I remember your face.
What happiness your letters.
I'm forever happy you are not with us.
I remember you always.
Happiness—happiness—what happiness—
three letters from you one after another!
What happiness that right now you are not with me.

7. P.S.

Starting today it's twelve months and eight days
until I see you again my little daughter, my dove.
....
Starting today it's ten years.
I was sentenced to ten extra years, my sweet girlkins.
The old sentence I've finished serving doesn't count.
With this I close this letter being as I am out of paper and fire.

When will we hold each other
unable to tear away?
"When they entered the apartment, it wasn't even plundered,
but—an old woman half-insane, half-alive."
Girl: unable to tear away.

ТАКСЫ

У профессора Д. было два сыновей
Нестерпимо серебряных синих кровей
И когда в Ленинбург подступила зима
Провожать их профессор надумал сама

Тот кто старше был в битву направлен легко
Уж назавтра им всем совершенно легко
Он летел озираясь как облакоКО
И шептал мне бы только открытКУ

послать
Чтобы ушла от порога нелепая мать
Что три года так станет стоять
Тот кто младше вернулся из битвы своей
Все же есть у меня еще чуть сыновей! —

Так воскликнул профессор, и стал языком
Его лоб обнимать, звать его дураком:
Ты так долго ходил мой единственный мой
А идти то всего то ты должен домой

Дом разрушен распался но это ничто
[Ты уже не узнаешь про то]
Сын последний не/и мертвый лежал не/и живой
Проплывал сквозь него этот окрик и вой:

Как Снегурочка таял, и таял и тлел,
Черный жемчуг, смарагд или лал.
Восемь месяцев тихо и гордо болел,
И еще полтора умирал.

DACHSHUNDS

Professor D has two sons
of such blue blood that the blood is silver.
Winter in LeninBURG
(brrr) time to address
the burning question
of wars. With a mouth
on their brows, Professor D
stamps her sons
to the borders of Leninburg.

The eldest has a blast.
By the next day,
light, relieved, he floats
cloudlike, and cants:
I just need to mail home a card
otherwise my silly father-mother
would wait forever by the door.

The youngest returns:
Brave Leninburg! BRRRRRR!
I do have a little bit of sons after all!
Professor fusses around him
with her loving tongue: silly child,
my one and only and gone so long,
go home now, our home is gone,
yes, our home is gone, go home.

Her son, no/more dead than no/more alive,
receives her howl into his human mold:
a snow maiden, he melts and molders,
ruby   black pearl   beryl.

И на город с высокого места смотрел,
Улыбаясь, его покидал:

—Слышишь/слышишь еще поживи/походи
Изнывающим шарканьем всех побуди
Ну не знаю собачку себе заведи
Прижимать к потрошеной груди

***

Постепенно в этом печальном доме завелось уже три
поколения такс.
«Я вошел в прихожую и навсегда запомнил открывшуюся
картину. Перед открытыми дверцами топящейся печки на
коврике лежала, правильнее всего сказать, «запеканка» из
такс и кошек. Их было, верно, по пятку каждого народца, и они
совсем перепутались. Где чьи лапы, где чьи хвосты,—разобрать
при этом освещении я не мог. Услышав стук двери и мои шаги,
одна из длинноухих головок поднялась и лениво тявкнула раз-
другой, потом упала на прежнее, очевидно, удобное и нагретое
место».

He is sick for eight quiet, proud months,
then he begins dying for another month and a half.
From a high point he bids
Leninburg a farewell:

Listen/listen live/trot a bit longer.
Keep neighbors awake with your sad shuffle.
What else ah there maybe get yourself a dog,
press it (grrr) to your disemboweled chest.

***

Eventually, three generations of dachshunds lived in this sad house.
"I would never forget what I saw when I entered the hallway. In
front of a hot Russian stove, on a rug, lay, let me call it, a casserole of
dachshunds and cats. There must have been about five of each kind
and they were completely tangled. In that bad light, I couldn't tell
between all the legs and tails. Upon hearing my steps and a knock on
the door, one long-eared head rose above the others, gave a lazy yap
and fell back to her spot that must have been cozy and warm."

ВСТРЕЧА

Солдат я был никудышный
—Николай Никулин

Она не знала своего отца
Она плохо знала своего отца
Когда он погиб ей было два года
Никакая весть не достигла
Осталась маленькая фотография
Очень светлое лицо
Разительное сходство
Впрочем фотография выцвела
77 лет спустя после его гибели она повстречала книгу
вздорную не желающую подчиняться не помнить
не желающую не видеть
какую заварили кашу
наверное вздорным был
ее тогда семнадцатилетний автор
эстет неженка и колючка
не погибший в населенном пункте
с подходящим названьем Погостье:
«Штабеля трупов у железной дороги выглядели пока как
заснеженные холмы и были видны лишь тела лежащие сверху
позже весной когда снег стаял открылось все что было внизу
у самой земли лежали убитые в летнем обмундировании
в гимнастерках и ботинках это были жертвы осенних боев
1941 года на них рядами громоздились морские пехотинцы в
булатах и широких черных брюках клешах выше—сибиряки
в полушубках и валенках, шедшие в атаку в январе-феврале
1942-го».
Она заложила это место маленькой желтой закладкой,
Решила все же со мной поговорить
Она спрашивает: ведь это мог быть он?
Ведь это мог быть и он там?
Ведь и он мог лежать там так?

ENCOUNTER

I was a worthless soldier
—Nikolai Nikulin

She didn't know her father
She didn't know her father well
She was two when he got killed in action
No notice followed
A small photograph remained
A face full of light
Stark resemblance
though the photograph faded over time
77 years after his death she met a book
A wayward book that refused not to remember
refused not to see
what pot has been stirred
Wayward must have been its seventeen-year-old author
a dandy, a snowflake, a porcupine
who didn't die at a rural rail station in Pogostie:
"Piles of corpses by the railroad looked like snowed-over hills and
only the bodies on top were distinguishable. In spring, once the
snow melted, the lower bodies emerged, dressed in summer uniforms,
soldier's shirts and boots. On top of them lay marines in heavy
leather jackets and black flared trousers. On top of the marines, in
short fur jackets and wool boots, lay the Siberians who launched
attacks in January–February of 1942."
She bookmarked this spot with a yellow scrap
and wanted to discuss it with me.
She asked: couldn't it be him?
Because couldn't he, right there?
Because couldn't he lie just like that?
What do you think?
Look here (her finger crashed into the letters):
We step over the corpses
We run over the corpses we hide under the corpses

Как ты думаешь?

Вот тут написано:

идем по трупам

перебегаем по трупам прячемся под трупами

как-будто так и надо

В тот момент,

Когда она это говорила,

Говорила и плакала от отвращения и радости встречи,

какая она была молодая какая красивая.

as if it were a common thing.
In that moment,
speaking and crying out,
disgusted and happy with this encounter,
how beautiful she was, how young.

СПРАВОЧНИК ЛЕНИНГРАДСКИХ ПИСАТЕЛЕЙ-ФРОНТОВИКОВ 1941–1945

От этих записей со мной происходит самоотравление
—Ольга Матюшина

1. Л. П. ПРИСУТСТВИЕ

Наша Маша

С ума сошла

Суровый Хармс вино пригубил

10 января: пороша, параша

Украли карточки!

Украли карточки!

Думаю—сам обронил

Сам себя пригубил,

Если бы не Маршак...

Лежишь на полу—рядом сладкой кишки крошка.

Лежишь на полу—рядом сладкая «Крошка Доррит»

Все помыкаются, попресмыкаются, конец будет делу венец.

Желудок жалобно подчиняется Диккенсу:

Ворчит, мурлыкает, блазнит, вздорит,

Живет магической, инфернальной жизнью,

Как в горе—мерцающий кладенец,

Как в горе—в самом нутре

Рождаются 2-3 слова

Но не просьбы, не жалобы, не угрозы,

Вылазят, выползают неудержимо—словно ночь из
    сердцевины дня,

Ты создал меня такого

Ты создал меня сякого

Только Тебе доверяю

Смотреть меня держать меня свежевать меня

A GUIDE TO LENINGRAD WRITERS, VETERANS 1941-1945

These records induce in me a self-poisoning
—Olga Matiushina

1. L.P. PRESENCE

Our Masha
brain-mashed
harsh Kharms kissed his wine
January 10: snow cap, shit can
Ration cards missing!
Ration cards missing!
Must have dropped them myself
kissed myself good-bye
if not for Marshak...
As you stretch on the floor next to bits of sweet guts
As you stretch on the floor next to sweet Little Dorrit
everybody twists, sucks up, ends well.
Mournfully, a stomach surrenders to Dickens:
grumbles   purrs   lusts   squabbles,
lives an enchanted infernal life
like a fairy sword inside a stone
like inside the starved—the curved—pain
2-3 words are birthed,
words not of request, not of complaint, not of threat
crawl out, unstoppable—like night straight from the day's heart:

Thou hast made me in Thy image
Thou've made me imagine that

only Thou I trust
to treat who Thou've made in your image
to trap who Thou've made in your image
to skin who Thou've made in your image

2. *О.Б. ГОЛОС*

Ангел но не голубой алый алый
Комсомолка Лили Марлен
С пуритански закушенной нижней губой
С небывалой
Плотской ясностью скул:
Во всём тебе удача!
Только разве вот незадача
НКВДшник выбивает из под тебя стул
(жирная лужа)
НКВДшник выбивает
Из тебя дитя,
Но и от этого тремоло энтузиазма
Практически не убывает.

15 января жирный ледяной туман, стужа.
Ты оставляешь в больнице
Юного нежеланного мужа
Умирать
И запыхаясь пыхтя
Тащишься на улицу Ракова
Мимо янтарных трупов и бирюзовых трупов
(«ах, какой художник всё это рисовал!»)

Твой новейший милёночек
Допрошает: где ты была?
Что бы об этом сказал Барков?
Что бы на это ответил Зубов?

Ну что ты такая?
Ну что это на тебе?
(какой бессмысленный ma chere искусительный карнавал)

2. O.B. VOICE

Angel not Blau Engel but Russia-red
Young communist Lili Marlene
with lower lip girlishly bit
and unprecedented
clarity of cheekbones:
girl, good luck!
In fact, tough luck:
NKVD man knocks a chair from under you
(a slop of grease)
NKVD man knocks
a child out of you
but doesn't stop
your enthusiastic thrash.

January 15: fog of grease, fog of bitter ice.
You leave a young unwanted
husband in the hospital
to die
and breathing heavily, drag
yourself to the Radio Bureau
by the corpses in amber, by the corpses in turquoise
(what artist colored them, what an eye!)

Your new guy
inquires: where've you been?
What would Barkov say about this?
What would Zubov say about this?

What's wrong with you anyway?
What's that on you?
(darling, what a queer triggering drag)

Выпуская ледяное яркое жало,
Ты лобызаешь его, ты погружаешься в микрофон,
Отстраняя сомненья
(не слишком ли быстро сюда бежала
покуда там от/до—ходил он?)

Нормально, не слишком быстро.
Твой высоконький голос
Проникает туда, куда другое ничто.

Сестры-братья мои!
Дочки-матери!
Я восхищаюсь вами насыщаюсь вами: утешаюсь вами
падая, падая, беспокоясь.

Что это на тебе?
Пальто Молчанова.

А что у нас под пальто?

3. В.В. И О.М. СЛУХ

Мордастый щекастый румяный царевич
Входит к слепой.
Молви она ему говорит,
Кто ты такой,
А ещё лучше пропой.

И он зачинает песню о жизни
О Кремле о морячках балтийских соболебровых
О земле, пропитанной подслащённой вшами
Слепая вздыхает блаженно
Как конь благодарно прядает ушами
Предрекает: от тебя будет толк,
Ибо ты нам напишешь блокадную оперетту.

Your stinger of ice hardens,
you drill a kiss into him, you bury yourself into a microphone,
you suppress doubts
(didn't you run here in one breath
while there he was breathing his last?)

No, you didn't.
Your high-pitched voice
penetrates where no other nothing.

Sisters-brothers of mine!
Mothers-daughters of mine!
I worship you, I watch you: I chirp
as I fall, as I fall and fuss.

What's that on you anyway?
Your husband's coat.

What have you got there under the coat?

3. V.V. AND O.M. HEARING

A faceful—a cheekful—a healthful of a prince
enters a blind woman's room.
Announce yourself, she orders,
and preferably with a song.

And he bursts into the song of life,
of the Kremlin, of young marines in the Baltic sable of beavers,
of his moist land sweetened with lice.

The blindwoman sighs with delight
moves her ears in gratitude like a horse
and predicts: you are the one
for you will compose Blockade the Musical.

Он говорит, извините, ослышался.

Она говорит именно-именно, мася моя,
С танцами-плясками, с шутками-прибаутками,
С героем-любовником в синем трико, обтягивающем чудеса,
С травести в пионерском галстуке, от экстаза дрожащем,
Там всё будет как настоящее,как в настоящем,
Но только в жанровой обработке.

Он говорит: чудеса!
Я готов слушать/слушаться тебя, слепая.
Расскажи мне
Что ты слышала этой зимой.

Слышала шорохи, шорохи запахи, засыпая
В смерть, слышала деликатное несъедобное прикосновение крыс,
Слышала краски острую сдобную вонь—голубая
Пахнет как Михаил Васильевич, синяя пахнет как
    Елена Генриховна,
Тень Гуро, насмешницы с овечьим лицом приходила сюда,
Я слышала её торжествующий топоток.

Город звенел скрежетал шептал щекотал (Каток на Елагином в
    детстве)
К шкафу прикручивлись коньки, в шкафу лежала моя
Безумица Мулюшка
Я катала-катала её по Большому проспекту
Там и оставила.
Из радиоточки как мёд как шёлк
как рыбий жир на нас текли
арии «Сильвы»,
Помнишь ли ты
Помню ли я
Помнишь ли ты
Помню ли я

Did I hear you right, he asks.

DA-DA-DA-darling, you heard me right.
A musical with bear-dances, catchphrases and punch lines,
with a male lead in tights, stretched over his private wonders,
a schoolboy shaking in ecstasy as a red scarf squeezes his neck,
it will be as fictional as our reality,
and in compliance with the demons of the genre.

Yes, blind comrade!
I'm ready.
Now you
tell me of the things you've heard this winter.

I heard rustle, rustle whiff, as I fell asleep
into death, I heard the gentle inedible dab of rats,
I heard the sharp delicious stench of paint—blue
that smells like Mikhail Vasilievch, violet that smells like
    Elena Genrikhovna,
Guro's shadow—Guro with a face of a sheep—came by,
I heard her triumphant pit-a-pat.

The city buzzed gnashed murmured tickled (a children's skating rink
    on Yelagin Island)
I bolted ice skates to the dresser where my
Insane Baby lay:
I wheeled her along Bolshoi Avenue
and left her there.
From the radio speaker, honey-like silk-like
fish-oil-like, arias from *Gypsy Princess*
streamed
Do you recall
Do I recall
Do you recall
Do I recall

Пусть это был только сон!
Но какой!
Ля-ля-ля.

4. В.В. И Н.К. ПАМЯТНИК

Мордастый бровастый румяный царевич
Входит к скупой.
На кой
Ты здесь лежишь?
Почему не бежишь?

За тобой присылали твои сыновья
Крутогруда обильна Большая Земля
Из сосков её пить Ленинградцы должны
И забыть-позабыть нехорошие сны

А куда мне бежать
Здесь все вещи мои
А куда мне бежать
Здесь все книги мои
Здесь все платья мои
Здесь все реки мои
Здесь все дети мои
Здесь две крысы мои:

Поль и Франц, притаились на полке сидят,
На собрание Чехова томно глядят,
Переписка суха фельетоны горьки,
Побрезгливей Суворина эти зверьки.

Никому никому
Не отдам не возьму
Ни вечернюю тьму, ни рассветную тьму,
Ни безумцев блокадных гы-гы и му-му,

Even if only dream!
What a dream!
La-la-la-la.

4. V.V. AND N.K. MONUMENT

A faceman, a healthman, a browman of a prince
enters the room of a miser.
Whyever
do you laze here?
Why aren't you on the run?

Your sons have sent for you
to beat off bad dreams
Leningradtchiks suck on the shaved
breasts of our Big Earth

Where should I go
All my goods are here
Where should I go
All my books are here
All my frocks are here
All my creeks are here
All my kids are here
All my two rats are here:

Paul and Franz transfixed on the shelf
dart glances at the collected Chekhov,
at that dry correspondence, bitter satirical shorts,
all more fickle than Suvorin, their picky editor.

Never ever
would I trade
this daybreak dark and this twilight dark,
the bah-bah, the moo-moo of the blockade cuckoo,

Ни прозрачную—bruit de silence—тишину
Перед взрывом, а после—в пыли и дыму
Остов бывшего дома на бывшем углу
Где читала тебя и тебе на полу.

Помнишь ли ты
Как улыбалось нам счастье
Помнишь ли ты
Помню ли я

Так оно и сейчас улыбается мне
И цинготные дёсны ему не закрыть.
Поль и Франц копошатся тревожно во сне
Надо встать потеплее малюток укрыть.

Как привольно в паучьем местечке моём!
Неразумный царевич, мы кротко живём,
И ни крохи былого не тратится здесь
Время вяло торжественно катится здесь
То вперёд то назад то вперёд то назад
Словно мяч по дорожке и листья чадят
То в Таврический Сад то в Михайловский Сад
И дистрофики гадят—и дети галдят.

5. В.И. ВОЗВЫШЕННОСТЬ

Я хочу есть как хочу творить
Я хочу творить как хочу есть.
Честно говоря, я не так уж хочу есть
Не так как они,
Приползающие к больнице, которой заведует мой муж,
Нервный неразговорчивый человек.
Я прохожу по двору больницы имени Эрисмана.

the see-through—bruit de silence—silence
before the blast, and later—the dust and smoke
over the skeleton of my ex-house on my ex-corner,
where I read you, where I read to you on the rug.

Do you recall
how happiness smiled on us
Do you recall
Do I recall

It smiles on me now
and cannot close its scurvy gums.
Paul and Franz are restless in their trance.
I should get up and tuck them in like two kids.

How tickled I am by this spider's nest!
Silly prince, we live humbly
we waste not a crumb of our past,
time rolls slowly like a triumphant tank
there and back, the bah and the moo,
like a ball in the park of burning leaves
from Tavrichesky Garden to Mikhailovsky Garden
while dystrophtchiks shit and the children shoo.

5. V.I. LOFTINESS

I want to eat as much as I want to write
I want to write as much as I want to eat.
On reflection, I don't really want to eat
not as much as them,
making their way to my jittery,
short-spoken husband's clinic.
I cross the front yard of a clinic named after F. Erisman.

В своей приличной лисьей шубке
С приличным перманентом цвета февральского пожара
На голове, украшенной глазками бусинками,
Красными от сострадания.

Я переступаю через них деликатно не тревожа не глядя.
Я прохожу через двор, у воротец
Переминается жмётся поэтесса Н.К.
Принесшая мне свой жемчуг.
Редкий красный

Ах что вы что вы сказала я
Взяла жемчуг
Нить истлела
Он посыпался
Отсыпала сахару
Он посыпался
Драгоценные! Драгоценные! кристалы.

***

Когда я пишу я взлетаю
Как джин
Кольца Маймун
Когда я пишу я взлетаю
Как джин
Лампы Дахнаш
Что угодно, господин?
Мне угодно сверху плыть
Между солнца между льдин
Где запретное свободно
Где вольготно превосходно
Где могущество и прыть
Где могущество и пыль
Разрушения и боя

In my decent fox coat,
with my decent hair the color of February flame,
with my decent hair pinned with googly beads,
Russia-red with compassion.

I step over them decently, disturbing not, looking not.
I cross the garden, by the gate
fidgeting, fingering her purse, I see poetess N.K.,
who has brought me her pearls.
Red, a rare find.

Oh you shouldn't have, I say.
I pick the pearls
Their thread is spent
The pearls spill
I trade sugar
Sugar spills
Precious! Precious! crystals.

***

When I write I soar
like a jinn from Maimun Ring
from the Dahnash Lamp. Master,
how can I serve you?
I wish to float amid
blocks of ice, amid blinks of sun
where the shut is shown
where gut is free
where force and speed
where force and dust
of combat and wreckage
the sky, blue-yellow white
needle grass and crass speech
greedy bite of a poetess miss odessa

Белизна и голубое с жолтым небо
И ковыль и корявый звук одесы
Жадный прикус поэтессы
Жалкий прикус поэтессы
Деревянная звезда
Я пишу и тают бесы
Бесстыдства и стыда:

Как хрупки льдинки эти
Однажды на рассвете
Тоску ночей гоня
От жажды умирая
В потоке горностая
Туда вошла она
Туда вошла Она
Туда вошла оня

needy bite of a poetess miss odessa
wooden star
I write and the demons melt
shameless demons melt
and ashamed demons melt:

Oh ice petal, no peace I find
the whole dawn through
sweetening my night
dying of thirst
I got an ice petal in my fur
oh oh she entered
oh oh She entered
oh oh shoo end

РАДОСТЬ

В.З.

Вот возвращается из/под шкафа давно оплаканная
  бесценнейшая копеечная серьга,
Веницейское стеклышко.
Виновато поблескивая
Сквозь пыль, как будто сквозь мех.
Допустим, Полина Анненкова, упавшая в темь/ в снега.
Просроченной жизни: кем ты будешь теперь?
Здесь уже все привыкли, что нет тебя на земле,
Поплакали да зачислили в сытный список потерь.
Читинская льдинка дурочка,
Будешь лежать в тепле
Моей ладони потом в уютной коробочке со своею парою,
Своею младшей сестрой,
Тоже несколько поцарапанной в ходе времени
Тоскою просто и по тебе тоской.
Теперь вас можно вынести в свет,
Чтобы каждая шептала мне на ушко:
«Как здесь светло и радостно и просто и хорошо».

JOY

to V.Z.

An earring returns, from under the cupboard, a bewept,
   priceless, pennyworth,
Venetian bauble.
Twinkling with guilt
through the dust or possibly fur.
Say, Polina Annenkova, cast into the murk/the snows,
is it moss or musings
of a life past due: what will you do now?
We've grown used to your absence on earth,
wailed and listed you among losses—a hearty list.
An ice chip in the Decembrist exile, a goofball,
you will lay in the heat
of my palm then in a cozy box next to your pair
your baby sis
also scratched in the transit of time
by plain yearning and yearning for a pair.
Now you can be carried into the light,
in my ear, the whisper of you:
"How bright and nice and plain and good."

ПЫЛКАЯ ДЕВА ИЛИ
ПОХОЖДЕНИЯ ЗИНАИДЫ Ц

ПРОЛОГ

Игорю Булатовскому

Автор обнаруживает в архиве публичной библиотеки им. Салтыкова-Щедрина акт о вскрытии в 1942 году командой библиотекарей и милиционером выморочной комнаты, ранее принадлежавшей Зинаиде Быковой, публиковавшей в начале века свои стихи и переводы из французской поэзии под псевдонимом Зинаида Ц., дальнейшие изыскания указывают, что репутация её как переводчика была настолько жалка, что только авторитет её мужа, выдающегося библиографа и библиофила, обеспечивал Зинаиде Ц. что-то вроде ниши в области изящной словесности.

A PASSIONATE DAMSEL, OR THE EXPLOITS OF ZINAIDA C.

PREFACE

to Igor Bulatovsky

In the Saltykov-Schedrin Public Library, the author discovers documentation of the 1942 authorized break-in—by a team of librarians and policemen—into the requisitioned room formerly belonging to Zinaida Bykova, an early-century poet and translator of French verse under the pen name of Zinaida C. Further research shows that her reputation as a translator was so piss-poor that only the authority of her husband, an outstanding bibliographer and bibliophile, provided Zinaida C. with a kind of a niche in the house of belle-lettres.

ФРАНЦУЗСКИЙ ЗАМО́К

Куда ушла Зинаида Ц.?
Вся вышла вытекла
(Вонючая темнота в яйце
Любителя блеска-нечисти похабника Фаберже)
Вытекла вся из квартиры-из комнаты-в доме-на этаже.

Сотрудники библиотеки и участковый составили акт
О том, что по вскрытии комнаты (два висячих и один
    французский замок)
Не посещавшейся покойной с января
В ней обнаружено.

Почему же покойная перестала посещать комнату?
Уж не разлюбила ли она все эти хорошие полезные вещи
Шкаф платяной двустворчатый
Кровать никелированную со старым ватным одеялом
Два небольших столика и пять стульев
Пейзаж и портрет П.В. Быкова в раме
Не верится чтобы покойная могла разочароваться в таких
    отличных вещах.

И главное—книги: на иностранных языках
Беспорядочно разбросанные
На столе на диване в шкафах в ящиках в корзинах на полу
Остатки архива первоклассные по своему значению автографы
Мопассан Мюссе Верлен

THE FRENCH LOCK

Where's Zinaida C.?
Gone from her eggshell
drained of its rotten darkness that leaked
from her room-in-the-apartment-on-the-floor-of-the-building
leaving behind the luxe of the naughty Fabergé.

A team of librarians assisted by a district police officer filed a report.
What they discovered upon breaking into the room (two hanging
    and one French lock)
which the deceased hasn't visited
since January—

Why did the deceased stop visiting this room?
Did she no longer love all these fine, gently used things?
An elegant double armoire,
a nickel-plated bed under a down quilt,
two medium desks, five chairs,
a landscape and a portrait of P.V. Bykov, framed.
It's hard to believe that the deceased could have grown disappointed
    in such excellent things.

Above all—books: in foreign languages
scattered
on the table sofa shelves boxes baskets floors,
scraps of the archive, first-class autographs,
Maupassant Musset Verlaine—

ОСТАТКИ АРХИВА

Нет, Сергунька, ну ты послушай.
—М.А.К.

««Скромность Зинаиды Ц. заключается въ томъ, что свои собственныя изліянія она пускаетъ въ плаваніе подъ флагомъ Мюссе и Верлена.

Объ этой книжечкѣ не стоило бы и говорить, если бы здѣсь не затрагивался вопросъ о переводахъ.

Желаніе публики познакомиться съ большими иноземными писателями такъ законно, такъ желательно, что всякая недобросовѣстность, малѣйшій обманъ въ этой области достоинъ самаго суроваго порицанія.

Полная невѣжественность, безмѣрная пошлость, явная недобросовѣстность въ обращеніи съ чужимъ имуществомъ, удивительная безпардонность—суть наиболѣе мягкія выраженія, какія мы можемъ употребить, говоря о переводахъ Зинаиды Ц.

Мы выражаемся мягко, не забывая ни минуты, что переводчица—дама.

Недобросовестность в обращении с чужим имуществом

Не забывая что переводчик дама
Бабуська девонька доча мама
(чья это она интересно мама?)
Не забывая что переводчица—яма
На Серафимовско-Пискарёвском,
Со ртом без вставной челюсти обмякшим.
Мы-то, Михаил Алексеевич не забываем,
Мы даже немного трепещем.
Вдовушка вдовушка лысая головушка
Золушка золушка с ваткой из ушка
Пни её ткни насквозь проткни
В стыд её слов как кутё в лужу жолтую обмакни.

SCRAPS OF AN ARCHIVE

Gosh, Serge, darling, listen to this.
—M.A.K.

"Zinaida C. is so humble that she releases her outpourings only
under the banner of Musset or Verlaine.
The sole reason to review this book in the first place is the issue
of translation.
The desire of the reading public to know great foreign authors is
totally legitimate and any small negligence, any little lie in that
respect deserves the most severe condemnation.
Complete ignorance, immense shallowness, reckless negligence
when handling this foreign property, shocking shamelessness—this
is the most generous description of Zinaida C.'s translations.
We take care to be courteous, keeping in mind at all times that the
translator is a damsel."

Reckless negligence when handling foreign property

Never forget that the translator is a damsel—
mumsy babushka devochka ovary
(whose mommy I wonder).
Never forget that the translator is a grave
at the Seraphim-Piskarev cemetery,
her sunken dentureless mouth.
Not only do we never forget, Mikhail Alexeyevich—
we are a touch struck.
Widow, widow, bald like a window.
Belle with a cotton ball in her ear.
Boot her blush her flush her face
into the shame of her words, like a yapper's mug into its piss.

Фу-фу!

Что за дряни ты натащила в строфу!

Желание публики познакомится с большими писателями
    так законно—

С чем это ты пигалица водворяешься на дракона?

Yuck!
What shit you've dragged into a stanza!
The public's desire to know great writers is totally fair—
How did you, little pimple, break out on the dragon's back?

IL BACIO

ПОЦЕЛУЙ ЭТО РОЗА ВОЛШЕБНОГО САДА
Baiser! Rose trémière au jardin de caresses!
Поцелуй! Мальвы цветок в саду объятья!

Мятой мягкой бумажной призывно-розовой
Мальвы торчком торчащий цветок
Персток
Указующий—
Поди сюда, щеголёк.

Выглядывающий из трав
Как иной уголёк
Выглядывает, подмигивая, из-под платья.
На каждый роток
Не накинешь свой звук, мелодию, хохоток.

Что же ты вдовушка не потрудилась раскрыть
Энциклопедию Botanica?
Вытянуть оттуда за круглый стебель
Но мальву, не розу, к мантильке-шляпочке приколоть?
Зачем отдала себя на растерзание заскучавшего умника,
Отдала себя перерезать-проредить-прополоть?

И куд-куда убежала потом
С этой копеешной розой волшебного сада—

В бомбоубежище, в очередь, за водой?
Я вижу остуствие твоё везде. Не надо
Не быть. А чё надо?—спрашивает она—что Вам надо?

IL BACIO

~~"A kiss is a rose of an enchanted garden"~~
Baisér! Rose tremièr au jardin de caresses!
A kiss! A mallow flower in the garden of embraces!

Come, you soft, crushed, dangling pink, a paper
pistil
of mallow, cocked
and pointing—
come here, little fella.

It peeps from the grasses
like ember
aflame, winking from under a skirt.
Could you cover every mouth
with a rhyme, a tune, a giggle?

Why did you, widowlette, fail to open
Encyclopedia Botanica,
to pull out of it a stem
not a rose but a mallow, a hollyhock, pin it
to your hat?
Why did you give yourself to be pulled to pieces by a bored critic?

Where did you charge to afterwards
with a penny rose from an enchanted garden—

to a bomb shelter, to a line for bread?
You are nowhere everywhere. Don't be
nowhere. Now what? she asks. What do you want?

ПРОЛОГ

Мне надо ляля тополя
Силы Добра и Зла
Силы Флобера Золя
Силы власти
Силы библиотэк
Превратить в один вот такусенький негаснущий кровоподтёк—

Вот эта старица
Где она умерла
Какого месяца числа
Какой прохожий
Прошёл мимо сугроба с ней, вмёрзшей.

Галошки торчали, как чернослив из свадебного торта.
Всё что подмалёвано, стёрто,
Я хочу проявить, обвести,
Как девочка—язык от усердия высунут—
Обводит заглавные буквы.

А эта какая буква?
А как ты думаешь?
У? Похоже на у.
Зинаида Быкова ложится в снег,
Как Верлен—в траву
На окраине Лондона.
Будь, что будет,
А я ещё поживу.

PREFACE

I want blah blah blah
and the power of yadda-yadda
the power of Flaubert and Zola
the power of good and evil
the power of libraries
So I could turn you into a chronic bruise
So I could clone you into a wound

This old witch
Where did she die
What month date
Which stranger
passed by the snowbank she was frozen into.

Her galoshes stuck out like two prunes on a wedding cake.
Whatever's touched up, wiped out
I wish to expose, to trace
like a child, her tongue sticking out studiously,
traces letters.

What letter is this?
What do you think?
Wooooooo Could be wooooooo
Zinaida Bykova lowers herself into the snow,
like Verlaine—into the grass
in a suburb of London.
I leave her now,
I live a bit now.

ХЭМПШИРСКИЙ АРХИВ. ПЕРСОНАЛИИ.

С рисунком Фроси Крофорд

I. ИНДЕКС

всё что ни сделаю бесстыдно иль абсурдно.
Богиня Бедности Воображения Судьбы подносит судно
Разряжена в звенящие шелка
На рукаве её зияет **Made in China**
А башмачки её трухи полны песка
По мне она жалка.
По мне—она необычайна.

II. ПРИЕЗД АННЫ

Китагава Утамаро. Самый конец Восемнадцатого века.
Предпочитал изображение ракушек изображению человека.

А когда уж ему приходилось включать изображения
детей-рыбаков-куртизанок в свои композиции,
То все они собирали ракушки.
Возбуждённые, продрогшие на ветру, краснолицые.

Блуждали в полных песка полосах прибоя
Извлекали оттуда удлинённые круглые плоские острые
     похожие на тюленье ушко.

На этой раковине расплёскано тревожное голубое
У этой оторвано крылышко—

Замечает чувствительная красавица, похожая на осьминога,
Другой красавице с длинной кроваво-красной раковиной в руке.
Та склоняет голову набок и смеётся: убога

HAMPSHIRE COLLEGE ARCHIVE. PERSONAE.

Art by Frosya Crawford

I. INDEX

Whatever's achieved sans sense and shame
Miss Goddess of Poverty Phantasy Fate hands a piss-pot
decked out in jingling silks
Made in China shines on her sleeve
her slippers full of dust, sand.
To me she is lame.
To me she is extraordinary.

II. ANNA'S ARRIVAL

Kitagawa Utamaro. The very end of the 18th century.
Preferred depicting seashells to human figures.

When he had to include the depictions
of children-fishermen-courtesans in his works,
he made them gather shells.
Stirred, chilled by the wind, flushed.

They roamed the sand-filled seashores
extracting   elongated   rounded   flat
sharp like a sea lion's flipper.

A jittery blue is spilled on this shell
A wing has been torn from that one—

says a sensual beauty who resembles an octopus
to another beauty with a long blood-red shell in her hand.
She tilts her head and laughs: cliched

Наша страсть реализовывать стыдливо створками
    придавленные метафоры.

Раковина твоя раковина полыхает в песке!!!!

III. АЛЛАДИН

Помутневший жестяной контейнер из-под молока
Содержит письмо Израиля Лихтенштейна,
Написанное в 1942ом году естественно.
Естественно в Варшавском Гетто
За две недели до его отправления в Треблинку.
Естественно.

Письмо гласит:
Я принимаю забвение для себя и своих близких
Моя жена (имя которой упоминать бессмысленно,
Пусть отныне будет она без-ымя-нна и без-лика)
Готова, стать жемчужной ниткой зубов,
прядью каштановой в матрасе, тенью.

Но нам бы было очень желательно,
Чтобы нашедшие эту жестянку с письмом помнили про нашу
    дочь—Маргалит.
Ей сегодня исполнилось двадцать месяцев.
О, это необыкновенный ребёнок!
Как, я вам доложу, она хорошо говорит

Гавалит гавалит гавалит
Gavalit Gavalit Gavalit

[Производит маленький гвалт]

is our love of embodying metaphors bashfully squished between
the valves.

Seashell your shell blazes in the sand!!!!

III. ALADDIN

A blackened milk tin
contains a letter of Israel Lichtenstein
written in the year of 1942 obviously.
Naturally, in the Warsaw Ghetto
two weeks before his departure to Treblinka.
Naturally.

The letter reads:
I accept oblivion for myself and for my loved ones.
My wife (whose name here is meaningless,
leave her be now nameless and faceless)
ready to become a pearl string of teeth,
a chestnut lock inside a mattress, a shadow.
Yet, we really wish
that whoever finds this letter inside a milk tin
remembers our daughter—Margalit.
Today she turns twenty months.
O, she's an extraordinary child!
Let me tell you, what a little talker, our Margalit

Gavalit Gavalit Gavalit
Margalit sp-*hic!* sp-*hic!* sp-*hic!*

[Margalit slits the margins of lit.]

Я обнимаю забвенье
Но я вас говорю:

IV. СЛУШАТЕЛЬ ОВЕЦ

Слушатель овец,
профессор когнитивистики,
седовласый красавец,
покуривает трубочку.

Он слушает овец,
Он ходит лишь туда,
Где движутся во тьме
Болтливые стада.

Средь клевера и пчёл и листьев златочёрных
Как радужный Адам до серого греха,
Он слышит средь овец особый склад стиха
Особых звуков смесь. Податливых? Упорных?

Я говорю ему: Что кроме беееее и мееее
Вы слышали от них?
Он отвечает мне,
Как в октябре, во тьме

Однажды он сидел,
Они стояли рядом.

«Я слышал тихий звон
Их тихих языков,
Как облако, тот звук лежал над сонным стадом,
Тот звук и звон, тот плеск, стеклянных башмаков».

I embrace oblivion,
but I speak you:

IV. SHEEP LISTENER

Sheep Listener,
Professor of cognitive science,
a gray-haired elf,
puffing on a slender pipe.

Hey, Mr. Sheeplistening Man,
beckoning beh-beh-beh-beh
from the quivering dark
are the whispering herds.

Amid clover, bees, and golden-black leaves,
like an iridescent Adam, before his gray sin,
he scans the sheep for a special way with verse,
for a compost of special sounds. Pliable? Tense?

I say: besides baa baa baa
what have you heard from them?
He tells me that once
in October, in the dark

he sat
and they stood.

"I heard a soft jingling
of their soft tongues
that sound—a cloud—rested over the sleepy herd,
that jingling and tinkling, that splashing, of glass slippers."

V. ХУДОЖНИЦА:

с недавнего времени я работаю с телом,
умирающим, стареющим, безобразным. Также меня занимает
тема нестандартной сексуальности и инцеста. Поэтому я
включила в экспозицию фотографии своего отца. Да, вот здесь
он уже совсем слабенький, атерсклероз, Альцгаймер...Слюна
течёт по щеке. В данный момент нахожусь в поиске новых
образов...
Замечание из зала: а здешняя природа вас вдохновляет?
Художница: природа?
Замечание из зала: у нас здесь знаете ли очень красиво
зимой. Деревья замерзают и на ветвях образуются прозрачные
наросты, ледяные шишечки. И через лёд чёрное видно. Вот бы
вы изобразили!
Художница: наросты? Шишечки? Ну не знаю...Не знаю...
Может быть.

VI. ИМЕНА ГОРОДОВ. KARA

Мне досталось сегодня немного тепла
Как снегурочка я над землей протекла
К удивлению бабки и дедки

Тучка-тучка, а вовсе не чёрный квадрат,
Я летела над сном массачуссетских хат,
Где машины живут и объедки.

Я летела над сыпью пустых городков:
Чикопи-Ничевог-Агавам.
Самый мёртвый из правивших здесь языков
Дал родиться клыкастым словам.

V. ARTIST:

Recently I've been working with a body,
dying, aging, ugly. I'm also interested in non-traditional sexuality and
incest. This is why this exhibit features photographs of my father.
Yes, here we can see him totally frail, atherosclerosis, Alzheimer's...
The drool of saliva across his cheek. Currently, I'm looking for new
ideas.
From the audience: does local landscape inspire you?
Artist: local landscape?
From the audience: It's really beautiful here in winter. The trees
freeze and crystal growths form over the branches, also icicles like
pine cones. And through that ice, the black shines. You could depict
that!
Artist: Crystal growths? Pine icicles? I don't know... don't know...
Maybe.

VI. NAMES OF THE CITIES. KARA

Today I was granted a bit of warmth
like a snow maiden I leaked above the earth
to the surprise of Grandfather Frost.

A cloudy-cloud, not at all a black square,
I flew above the sleep of the Massachusetts huts,
filled with machines and leftovers, I flew

above the rash of empty towns:
Chicopee-Nichivogue-Agawam.
The deadest of all the languages reining here
pushed out fanged words.

Я летела над чёрною связью дерев,
Занесённых над серой травой.
Там река издавала мучительный рёв
Чуть подальше отчаянный вой.

Как зовут вашу реку? Коннектикут. Врут.
Имя ей — разложившийся вчернь изумруд
В блеклой пене и мутной парше —
Как прелестница с мёртвым ребёнком в душе.

Как зовут вашу зиму?
Никак не зовут.

I flew over the black truss of trees
in the gray grass.
There, the river let out a bitter roar
and further—a roar of despair.

What is the name of your river? Connecticut. Liars.
Its name is a decomposed emerald,
pale foam and muddy scab—
like a bride with a dead child in her heart.

What is the name of your winter?
None.

РЫБА

Ирине Сандомирской

За всё это время
За всё это время
Мне было выдано два часа покоя
Время расступилось и пропустило меня
Катька надела на меня маску, приделала ко мне трубку
И сказала: плыви.
Я поплыла и увидела, что это такое.

Одно за другим появлялись огромные лица рыб
С таким же как у меня ртом.
Рыба слеза рыба коза рыба вы все угадали правильно стрекоза
Рыба моль рыба узник

Но ближе всего к моему лицу подплыла рыба старуха
Thalassoma ballieui
Непонятно, была ли она самец старуха или самка старуха
Небольшое серое животное
Молодые старухи переливаются нежными красками
В зрелости старухи мутнеют
Рыба старуха единица моего времени
Времени моего контейнер
Двигалась вдоль коралла прожирая его насквозь
Я же двигалась за ней, обдирая о риф локти и колени
Мы были одно.
О дно
Ударилась рыба и стала птицей.
Рыба птица приблизилась к рыбе старухе.
Они недолго там поделили молчанье о сем, о том,
      повисели рядом,
Держась за скользкую, твёрдую выпуклость рифа

THE FISH

to Irina Sandomirskaya

All this time
All this time
Allotted me two hours of peace
Time has parted in front of me
Katie strapped a mask onto my face, attached a tube
And said: swim
And I swim and see what it's like

One after another huge fish faces appear
Mouths identical to mine
Fish tear drop fish nanny goat fish dragon boat
fish moth fish yard bird

Nearest to my face swims an old woman wrasse
Thalassoma ballieui
Whether she is a male old woman or a female old woman
   remains unknown
A small gray beast
Young old women are iridescent
With age they go dim
An old woman wrasse is a unit of my time
A storage unit of my time
Gorges through coral riffs, behind it
I move scraping my elbows, knees
We are one
The fish bangs
Itself on the bottom
And turns bird
Fish bird nears fish old woman
They exchange silences, hang together
Holding on to the hard, slippery reef

Голодным и сильным ртом.

....

Каждое утро

На острове

Я просыпалась от страшного, возбужденного хора птиц.

О, как страшно кричали они о

Наступлении нового дня.

With their strong, hungry mouths
....
Every morning
On the island
I am woken by a horrid, excited choir of birds
How horridly they scream
Greeting a new day.

МИЛОСТЬ

В этой сказке выпало мне подработать Шахерезадой,
Горькоглазой темноязыкой угрюмозадой,
Полной песка и пепла песка и пепла,
Но по мере свивания текста выросло и окрепло
Тело моих скитаний, презентабельным стало скисло
В горечь речь простокваши,
Исполнилось квази смысла.

Шахрияр, не казни меня!

Не потому что тоже,
Как и сотни других, я искала тебя на ложе,
Утоляя бореньем воли ночные страхи,
Не потому, что мне неохота плахи
Вонь почувствовать лезвия и прощанья негу,

Не казни, потому что со мной по снегу
(что это «снег»? Он любопытствует, но, скорее, вяло)
Ты уйдёшь;

Как старое одеяло,
Снег в моем краю желтоват, сероват, следами
Испещрён неведомыми.

Как после пожара в дыме
Все хлопочут уже ненужные миру тени,
Снег в моем краю—
Обрамленье предел хотений:

Не казни меня.

MERCY

In this story I moonlight as a bitter-eyed
Scheherazade, a dark-tongued, grumpy-
bootied Scheherazade, full of sand
and ash-sand and ash,
as the story spins, my body grows harsh
hard body roams grows presentable sour
milk of speech
ferments into quasi senses.

Shahriar, sentence me to mercy.

Not because like the rest of them
searching for you between sheets and pillows
I wrestled my night fears inside the cuddle of wills.
Not because I'm averse to climbing a scaffold,
to the stink of a blade, the affections of the last goodbyes.

Sentence me to mercy because across the snows
(flaccidly he asks, What is this "snow"?)
I would lead you away from here;

like a worn blanket,
snow in my empire is yellowed, gray, marked
with mysterious tracks.

Like, in the smoke, after a house fire,
dead shadows are still trying to reach for safety,
snow in my empire frames
the end of desire:

Mercy, Shahryar.

Пока я говорю
О вулкане-рыбе,
О вагине подземной, которая вход в Магрибе
В усыпальницу демонов,
О кошке, царице яда,

На тебя проливается морок печаль услада
Утешение,
Вот ты и слово и вот ты снова
Белый сонный младенец,
Всему основа в тёплом доме, что только тобою дышит,
Пёс храпит, повивальник вышит,
Бабка гладит лицо твоё, мудрая и живая,
От несносной нежности подвывая.

Я ещё говорю:
Не казни меня.
Лал сияет,
Слово невысказанное зияет,
Как жемчужину в рот тебе положу за щеку.
Как себя в огонь твой,
чтоб длился,—
Бумажку щепку.

As I speak
of a fish that erupts like a volcano,
of an underground vagina that leads straight to Maghreb, into a tomb
   of demons,
of a feline tsarina of poison,

You sit in the way of sorrow, grief, pleasure,
solace
you are a word you are a white
dozing newborn,
a backbone of a warm house, its breathing.
A dog snores, swaddle blankets embroidered,
Grandmother, wise and living, touches your face,
howling out of unbearable tenderness.

I repeat once more
Have mercy
A ruby flares
A word, unsaid, flares
under your cheek, I tuck
—as if putting my body into your fire
to keep it going—
a paper chip   (a pearl)   a wood chip.

ПУБЛИЧНАЯ БИБЛИОТЕКА
В САН-ФРАНЦИСКО

Илье Каминскому

На развале в библиотеке.
Роюсь в старых картах
Мест не вызывающих
Никаких воспоминаний
Никаких предчувствий
Всё здесь можно купить за медные деньги
Любую местность
Пригорки, дюны, болота, вереск, поворот направо.
Вдруг замечаю компетицию, оживленье:
Рядом с моей рукой
Появляется другая, точная и хищная рука.
Длинные грязные ногти, бордово смуглая кожа, синячки
     на венах.
Пальцы, как будто читая азбуку Брайля,
Оглаживают на карте
Железнодорожные насыпи,
Сыпь населённых пунктов
И вдруг я слышу подземный голос:
Потрогай это
Я говорю: извиняюсь?
Потрогай эту бумагу
Думаю врут никакого она не 1864 года, а позже:
Слишком ровная, слишком молодая.
Берёт мою руку в свою руку
Подносит мой палец к обрезу страницы
«Совершенно очевидно что это новьё:
Резали толсто, грубо, торопились».
В раздражении выходит,
Уносит запах гниющей плоти, наркотика, моего изумленья.

THE PUBLIC LIBRARY IN SAN FRANCISCO

to Ilya Kaminsky

At a library sale
I sift through old maps
of places that stir
neither memory
nor calling
for pocket change you can buy it all
any region
hills, dunes, bogs, heather, a turn to the right.
Suddenly I sense competition, a challenger:
next to my hand
another hand appears, greedy, vulturous,
dirty long nails, vinous skin with bruised veins.
Fingers, as though reading Braille alphabet,
fondle the map's
railroad embankments,
a rash of towns,
suddenly I hear an underground voice:
"Touch this"

Excuse me?

"Touch this paper
It cannot be from 1864, they are lying." Then:
"Too even, too fresh."
He takes my hand into his,
brings my finger to the blade of the paper
"Obviously new:
see how thick, how rough the cut, as if done in a rush."
Annoyed he leaves,
with him, he takes the smell of rotting flesh, drugs, my astonishment.

МУТАБОР

О.К.

1. MADRE INFELIZ

В моей жизни образовались дыры
Которые мы символически можем определить как «субботы»
    и «воскресенья»
Я пыталась заполнить их твоим языком
Твоим глазом, твоим смехом, твоим членом
от этого заполненья наступала смерть.
Но на смену смерти приходило воскресенье—и это
    было плачевно.
Я пыталась заполнить их твоим голосом то
отрицающим то отпевающим то отпивающим меня
как горькое горящее полезное зеленоватое пойло.
Когда меня становилось меньше,
Мне становилось легче.
Я пыталась их заполнить Беседой.
Я пыталась их заполнить Наблюдением
жирным сурком бледным нарциссом безжалостной старухой
Но через дыры в меня наплывало
Зияние блистанье мерцанье
Даже называнье—
«она отдает дочь на выходные отцу»—
Блокировало усыпляло
ядовитое светящееся
в меня облако
лишь частично.
Я скребла пол ногтями
Я сидела смотрела во тьму
Я кусала ногти
Я сидела считала часы
Я ощущала себя несколько неадекватной
Я звонила подруге

MUTABOR

to O.K.

1. *MADRE INFELIZ*

My life has given way to the gaping cracks
which, for the sake of speech, I'd call "Saturdays" and "Sundays."
I tried to fill them with your tongue
your eye your laughter your penis
this infilling led inevitably to death.
But death was followed by Sunday's rising—poor me
I tried to fill it with your voice that
either cancels or channels or samples me
like booze, bitter burning green
when I shrank
it felt good
I tried to fill them with Conversation
I tried to fill them with Observation
with a fat groundhog a pale narcissus a merciless hag
But, through the gaping cracks came over me
a shining, a glittering, a twinkling
the very act of naming—
"on weekends, her daughter's father has the custody of their child"
blocked, sedated
a poisonous, shining cloud
inside me
only partially
I clawed the floor
I sat & stared into the dark
I bit nails
I sat&counted hours
I felt rather inadequate
I called a girlfriend

Подруга наливала молоко из груди в рот своей девочке
Как из лейки
убаюкивая меня как-
нибудь обойдется
Займись делом
Я занималась делом
Кора моя простодушная Деметра
Ты набивал мой рот гранатовой кашей
Горели зёрна
Пальцы твои погружались в мой рот как бороны в землю
Когда она на землю вернется
Будет понедельник

2. ДРУЖЕСТВЕННЫЙ РАЗВОД

На некоторой стадии своих супружеских отношений
Я стала ходить ночевать
К местному автору Эмили Дикинсон
То к дереву возле ее дома
То на кладбище.
Почему зачем-то чему
Именно туда?
Во-первых, мне было стыдно ходить туда где другие люди:
мама, либо бездомные, либо кто угодно.
Во-вторых, мне нравилась твердая земля и твердые корни
Вроде как секс.
В-третьих я люблю поэтов
Живых, но еще
Лучше мертвых
Мертвые поэты любят меня
Эмили в нестираной ночной рубашке пахла рыбой
Сначала, когда я стала там лежать мне было страшно
Январь (хотя и теплый)
Но потом выяснилось что ничего страшного:
Экстатика

The girlfriend was pouring milk from her breast
as if from a watering can into her girl's mouth
lulling me ok
ay
keep busy
I kept busy
Kora, my simple-hearted Demeter,
you filled my mouth with pomegranate kasha
seeds on fire
your fingers buried into my mouth like harrows.
When she comes back up
it will be Monday

2. A FRIENDLY DIVORCE

At a certain stage of my spousal relations
I took up spending nights at a local
author's, Emily Dickinson's,
either under a tree by her house
or at the cemetery.
Why were these particular
places chosen?
Firstly, I was ashamed of going to popular spots
frequented by my mother or the homeless or whomever else.
Secondly, I liked hard earth and hard roots
A kind of sex
Thirdly, I love poets
Living and particularly
Dead
Dead poets love me back
Emily in an unwashed nightgown reeking of fish
In the beginning I was afraid to lie down there
January (but rather warm)
Then it turned out to be just fine
Ecstacy

Катарсис
Кончишь в землю ан не замерзнешь.
После того, как вывернешь себя воплем наизнанку,
Так что внутренности качаются,
Как моллюски прилипшие к кораблю.
Хорошо лежать на земле.

Впоследствии я познакомилась с человеком,
питающим слабость к кладбищам
Отведи меня туда-туда
сказал он
Ведь может случиться и так, что я никогда не вернусь
А не хотелось бы уезжать не увидев

3. МУТАБОР

Аист аисту летит
Аист аисту кричит
Неубитого живого!
Дай давай разбудим слово!

Казалось бы какие только слова
Они не испробовали на вкус не использовали на звук
На прочность.
Живые слова, мертвые слова
Слова своих родителей безобразные слова своих старших сестер
Они заполнили себя словарями синонимов рифм
Технических и медицинских терминов
Непристойностей и имен
Слова с нестерпимым звуком со свистом проносились мимо
Оставляя нас пустыми но недоудовлетворенными

Catharsis
Orgasm into the ground to keep it warm
After a howl turns your insides out
tossing your guts like
barnacles on a boat
how good to lie on the ground

Consequently, I met a man
with a weak spot for cemeteries
"Take me there there there,"
he said
"It could happen that I'd never come back here again
I don't want to leave without seeing"

3. MUTABOR

Stork-a-stork, a burning flame
in the forest of your name.
Killed not, killed not, killed not stork!
Dare we stir a word to work?

What words they haven't tongued, haven't
stalked from book to branch, haven't sucked
like a raven a worm, these storks
thrashing their beaks, probing the strength
of sounds, of living words, dead words,
words of their parents, ugly disfigured words of their
elder sisters, they stuffed themselves with the dictionaries
of synonyms, rhyme dictionaries,
technical and medical lexicon,
dirty words and proper nouns,
words flew by us with their exhausting swish,
leaving us empty, sub-satisfied.

Мы шли ночью
Мое сердце дрожало как новорожденный крысенок
Желанный жалкий зимний приплод
Вывалившийся на тугие брусничные листья
Скрипящий как корень мандрагоры
Мы ждем перемен сказал ты
С ледяною насмешкой Пьеро-то-ли-Арлекина
Мертвый поэт М. Семенко на краю земли
Пишет тьмы кричащих стихов.
Живой поэт Александр С. ходит по Амхерсту
Машет длинными руками: калиф-аист, оценивает, смеется.

Нет: мы ждем перерожденья
Они испробовали все слова
Какие только приходили им на ум:
И муртобор, и мурбутур, и мурбурбур, и муртубур.
Но ничто не помогало,
Заветное слово навсегда исчезло из памяти,
И они как были,
Так навсегда и остались аистами.

We walked at night.
My heart shivered like a newborn rat,
a wished-for, woeful, winter infant
that has dropped into thick redberry leaves
screeching like the mandrake.
We are waiting for change to come, you said coldly.
A dead poet, M. Semenko, on the edge of the earth in Vladivostok
writes darknesses of screaming poems.
A living poet, Alexander S., walks all over Amherst,
waves his long arms: a Caliph Stork.

No: we are waiting for a transformation.
They have tried all the words they could
come up with:
murtobor, murbutur, murburbur, murtubur.
Nothing worked.
The magic word of the spell has vanished from their memory
and they remained, as they were, storks.

ЛЮБОВНЫЕ ПРОГУЛКИ ПО ГОРОДСКИМ КЛАДБИЩАМ

О.К.

1. GREENWOOD, BROOKLYN

Около слезообразного прудика—в основном итальянцы.
Их склепы приподняты отлажены
Как новенькие вставные челюсти,
Их склепы выпячивают свои азалии, сирени, бугенвилии,
Мокрые кусты как мокрые тела натурщиц на сером
    допустим шолке—
Развлечения старых фамилий.
Зато в колумбарии кого только нет

Тут тебе и сдержанные китайцы,
и некто с таким простым русским именем,
На полочках урночки, вазончики, буковки,
Фотографии лысых людей в шортах.
Потертый ковер несвежее кресло—
Сиди себе помни о смерти.
Но главное жирные нежные рыбы
Золотом текущие
В черной блестящей воде—
(смерте-уха):

Ты смотришь на рыб
На трепещущий воздух
Ты медлишь
Ты торопишься
Пойдемпойдем

ROMANTIC WALKS THROUGH CITY CEMETERIES

to O.K.

1. GREENWOOD, BROOKLYN

By a tear-shaped pond: mostly Italians.
Their crypts are vaulted, polished
like brand-new dentures,
their crypts puff out their azaleas, lilacs, bougainvillea -
the nude bodies of bushes pose on marble silk—
dead old gents don't abandon their favorite pastimes.
The columbarium, however, offers diversity.

Here you got the discreet Chinese,
there, a name that out-Russians all Russians,
on the shelves—diminutive vases, letters, urns,
photographs of bald people wearing shorts.
A worn rug, an old armchair—
sit all you wish and memento mori.
But this fish here—this fat, silken fish
this gold-float
in shining black water -
(the fishy broth of death):

You observe the fish
the trembling air
you linger
you rush
letsgogogo

Здесь лежит Mary O'Brian 38 лет
Здесь ее дочка Lily
Двух лет
Mary еще пожила после дочки
Еще погуляла
башмаками поцокала
Зонтик пораскрывала в бруклинский дождь
Ртом повздыхала
А потом все же подле своей Лили прилегла
Успокоиться.

Я приближаюсь к ним
Запинаюсь и падаю
Хорошо еще что не на камень
Ты говоришь ну что же ты
Неуклюжая
Отряхиваешь мою одежу
От дорогой похоронной земли.

2. NEW ORLEANS, ST. LOUIS CEMETERY ≠1

«С 15-го марта можно посещать только тургруппами»

А то знаете ли трогают где попало
Лапают в запретных местах
Воруют камни
Испражняются на саркофаги
Пытаются заселять склепы и мавзолеи.
Как это устроено:

В домике дверца
раз в месяц она открывается,
Туда как хлеб
Помещается мертвец.
Через месяц (на самом деле—

Here lies Mary O'Brian, 38 years old
Here her daughter Lily, 2,
Mary did live a nick after her daughter
did some moving-on
did some clip clop clip clop with her heels
click-opened her umbrella in the Brooklyn rain
sighed a few more times with her mouth.
Finally lied down by her Lily
to rest.

I near them
I stumble and fall
"At least not on a stone"
you say "what's wrong with you
clumsy"
you brush off my clothes
sweet sweet funereal earth

2. NEW ORLEANS, ST. LOUIS CEMETERY #1

"Starting March 15th the cemetery is open only to tour groups"

Because they come: all fingers, all eyes,
start touching the untouchable
steal stones
relieve themselves onto sarcophagi
settle down in crypts and mausoleums.
This is how it works:

Once a month, inside a tiny house
a door opens and into it
bread-like
a deadman is thrust.
In a month (in truth,
much sooner

Гораздо раньше,
Но месяц—срок уважения)

Можно подселять следующего
Никакой толчеи
Никакой коммунальности.
Только пепел!
Такая жара!
Пейте пейте не забывайте пить!

Не забывайте пить:
Бурбон мята ром сахарная пудра
Такая жара
Пот вирус лихорадка химера

Теннеси Уильямс деловито разглядывает юного трубача
Юный трубач деловито разглядывает Теннеси Уильямса
Оба посасывают кусочки льда, оба определяют цену.

Хищный винт кондиционера
Режет влажный жар
Ломтями
На твое бледное потное лицо
Лопасти нарезают черные тени

Кто же здесь упокоен?
Преуспевшая жрица вуду, ценимая за услуги властями города,
Выживший из славы, но не из интереса к недвижимости актер,
Заранее подыскавший себе местечко в тени,
Гостеприимный склеп покуда пустует,
А в склепе попроще: неимущие трубачи,
Те сгорают свое
За деньги местной миллионерши,
Пожелавшей остаться известной.

but a month is a term of respect),
a roommate moves in.

No need to be cramped,
this is not an apartment in Leningrad.
This is pure hundred percent ash!
We are brewing.
Drink drink don't stop drinking.

Don't stop drinking:
Bourbon mint rum powdered sugar
We are brewing
sweat virus fever chimera

Tennessee Williams contemplates a young trumpeter
A Young Trumpeter contemplates Tennessee Williams
Both suck on ice shavings, both wonder about the price

The predatory blade of a fan
slices humid heat
onto your salted face
Blades cut black shadows

Who is resting here?
A well-to-do voodoo priestess, favored by the authorities,
an actor who lost his fans but not his fondness for real estate
and reserved himself a shady spot in advance,
a welcoming crypt stands empty,
next to it, in a modest crypt: broke trumpet players
burn
with financial assistance from a local billionaire
who wished to remain known.

3. ГОД СПУСТЯ. ЛЬВОВ. ЛЫЧАКОВСКОЕ КЛАДБИЩЕ

Начало сумерек
Подкрашивает серо/оранжевым
Расползшиеся, высыпавшие
По всему кладбищу
мелкие розы,
Не случайно:
Первых покойников кладбища
Принесла сюда именно бубонная чума.

«Защитники Львова—
Молодые орлята»,
погибшие прямо здесь на кладбище
упрямые подростки,
Защищавшие древние могилы
В непосредственной близости
от своих будущих могил.

Позвольте, позвольте
Защитники Львова от кого?
Кто только ни наступал
Кто только ни покушался
Кто только ни вкушал
Ни желал поглотить
и впитать.

«Повстанцы 1863-го» покоятся в своем квартале,
А «ноябрьские повстанцы» в своем.
Это гордые твердые кварталы.
Также отведены места для тех,
кого вынесли из городской тюрьмы

(священников, например, Советы в миметическом
    порыве распинали),
для тех, кто присоединился к «Галичине».

3. A YEAR LATER. LVIV. LYCHAKIV CEMETERY

Early dusk
paints gray/orange
the edges of the spilled
miniature roses
not by chance:
the first dead men arrived to this place
during the bubonic plague.

"Defenders of Lvov—
young eagles."
They perished right here in the cemetery
stubborn youths
who stood up to defend ancient graves
next to their own
future graves.

Hold on
Defenders of Lvov from who?
But who didn't entrench
But who didn't usurp
But who didn't soup and salad
here wishing to swallow
to absorb

"The 1863 Insurgents" rest in their quarters,
while "the November insurgents"—in theirs.
Hard proud quarters
shared with those
dragged out of the city prison

(priests, for instance, often crucified by the Soviets in a mimetic gesture),
or those who joined "The West Ukrainian People's Republic."

Эти могилы смотрят на меня, улыбаясь,
Как нищий у входа со своей веселой культей.
Спрашивать, что именно привело его сюда—не бестактно ли?

Всюду могилы актрис,
их мужей, томных польских адвокатов,
их любовников, взвинченных украинских журналистов.
Арт деко.
Немного похоже на пирожные в местных тесных кондитерских.
Круглоглазая муза Пуччини с голосом глубоким и темным, как
    зеркало,
Обмелевшим, ушедшим в землю как здешняя река.

Во время немецкой оккупации несравненная Madame Butterfly
Побиралась на рынке.
Гнилые капустные листья нежные как шелк перчаток дивы.
Она замолкла.
И ты замолкаешь.

Это кладбище молчания.
Кварталы кладбища молчат с кварталами.
Передо мною любопытное молчание:
Так молчат после боли и после любви.

4. КЛАДБИЩЕ МАУНТ ХЕБРОН, КВИНС, МОГИЛА ДОВЛАТОВА

Покойся милый прах:
Участок 9, линия 14,
Среди жарою разоренных птах
И белок самовитых.
Среди фамилий знаменитых
Банкиров, адвокатов с одышкою
Их жен с базедою,
Их жарких дочерей.

These graves follow me with a smile
of a beggar leaning on a stick by the entrance.
The question: what has brought you here? seems rather tactless.

I'm surrounded by graves of actresses,
their husbands—beefy Polish lawyers,
their lovers, disgruntled Ukrainian journalists.
Art deco
somewhat resembles cakes in crammed local bakeries.
A round-eyed Puccini's muse with a voice deep and dark like a mirror
that later dried up and disappeared into the ground like a local river.

During the German occupation
the incomparable M-me Butterfly
floated with her begging wing in the market.
Rotten cabbage leaves, soft like silk gloves of a diva.
She grew silent.
You follow.

This is a cemetery of silence
a silent togetherness of the earth.
I'm pinned by this strange silence
post-pain, post-love.

4. MOUNT HEBRON CEMETERY, QUEENS, SERGEI DOVLATOV'S GRAVE

Rest in peace, darling dust:
Plot 9, line 14,
among birds ruined by sunshine,
among self-sufficient squirrels,
the household names of bankers,
lawyers with shortness of breath,
their wives with Graves' disease,
their hot daughters.

Как пусто, как светло,
Как раскаленною зарей
Подсвечено отсутствие тебя.
Далекой битвы пересмешник,
Судья безжалостный в бессовестной игре.

Поди ж любой из нас «меж датами тире»,
Но ты не то. Ты точка, окончатель текста,
Что дикий город из себя истек.
Проживший все его неловкие причуды:
Пастушью сумку в мертвом доме,
Горький хлеб ненужных языков,
Тщеславия тиранящий искус.
Ты здесь? Так сказано на камне.
Огромный мертвый Карабас,
Брезгливыми и ловкими руками
Нас превративший в нас.

Велевший ничему не верить, кроме слова,
Ничтожеству играться своему,
Издать себя желавший, как «муму» —
Герасим, — жадно. Толку не создавший
На топях Ленинграда,
Здесь зато
Изрядно преуспевший, опоздавший
Лишь под скальпель кардиолога. ЛИТО
Небесное ему должно быть радо.

Там наверху он нравы их чернит,
Их этим самым смерти изымая,
Блондинок смотрит, мальборо чадит,
Зачеркивает буквы и чертит,
Рука его болит, в предплечии немея.

What light, what emptiness
compose this sizzling dusk
that now illuminates your absence.
A smartass general of distant battles,
a ruthless judge in a dishonest game.

Of us they say "a dash between two dates,"
but not of you. You are a full stop, a period
at the end of a text this wild city squeezed out of you.
A city whose whims you've braved:

a shepherd's bag in the house of the dead,
the bitter bread of superfluous tongues,
the tyrannical trial by vanity.

You here? The stone says so.
A corpse-puppeteer
whose deft, squeamish hands
have written us out of us.

Your advice: have faith in nothing but words,
have fun with your worthless little self.
Your greed: to get oneself published.
Having accomplished nothing of worth
in the marshes of Leningrad,
you've turned the trick here, arriving late
only under the scalpel of a cardiologist.
Creative workshops of heaven rejoice upon your arrival.

There, your mere rebuke of their morals
is suffice to lift them out of infamy,
you study blondes, smoke Marlboros,
your hand crosses out words, crosses lines
all while being dead at the shoulder.

СЕМЬЯ
БЕГСТВО В ЕГИПЕТ

Т.П.

О как они ненавидят друг друга в этой пустыне
Как неизбывно и безнадежно
Как тяготятся привычками:

Мария дергает носом как кроль
Розовым вечно предпростуженным—
Как жемчужина
Речная дешевая.

Иосиф откашливается в конце предложений,
Как будто смеётся.
Но, поверьте нам, он не смеётся,
Не до смеха ему.

С тех пор как явилась весть
И стало понятно,
Что, как многоголовое чудовище, они связаны:
Затхлыми яслями
Болтовней волхвов
Тяжестью
Блестящею
Дешевизной их ненужных даров
Ее провалинкой рта морщинистым лицом пытающимся
    отвернуться от креста,
Смотреть куда угодно
Да хоть вдаль
В пустыню.

Темный холодный песок:
В семье это счастье— не быть собой,

FAMILY
FLIGHT TO EGYPT

to T.P.

They are done with each other in this desert.
No-turning-back done, damn done.
Done with all those little habits:

Maria always twitching her rabbity nose
chronically pink and running—
a pearl of a nose,
fresh-water, of little value.

Joseph coughs at the end of each sentence
as if bursting into laughter
but trust us, he isn't laughing,
there is nothing to laugh about.

Since the annunciation
it became clear
that, like a many-headed beast, they are one:
a moldy cradle,
chatty Magi,
the heavy, gold
cheapness of their useless gifts.
The cliff of her mouth,
a wrinkled eye avoiding the cross.

To look anywhere,
there, into the distance,
there, into the desert.

Black, cold sand:
in a marriage, what happiness it is not to be oneself,

Не знать себя,
Следовать за другим,
Утешаться малыми слабыми приступами
    брезгливости раздражения,
Мечтой о бегстве.

Ирод зияет вдали как тяжкое грязное облако
Или как злодей в фильме Сергея Иосифовича Параджанова
(угадывается автопортретнре сходство)
Ослик уныло трюхает
Глаза его жолты губы напряжены.

Мария хныкает тихо тоненько.
Притворяется?
Иосиф оглядывается,
Нежеланная жалость к жене и чужому ребёнку пронзает его.

Звезда вот-вот вылупится:
Наглая благоуханная
    как первый весенний цветок.

not to know oneself,
to follow the other,
to be comforted with little, attacks of squeamishness, surges
    of irritation.
With dreams of escape.

Herod gapes in the distance like a heavy dirty cloud
or a villain in a film by Sergei Parajanov (uncanny resemblance).
A donkey is bored,
its eyes yellow, smackers stiff.

Maria is quietly weeping.
Faking it?
Joseph looks around, pierced
with an unwelcomed pity for his wife and a child not his.

Like the first flower of spring,
bold, fragrant,
the star is about to hatch.

ЧУЖОЕ ПИСЬМО

Куртавенель, среда.
Вчерашний день был менее однообразен, чем позавчера.
Мы сделали большую прогулку,
А когда вернулись, великое произошло событие.
Вот что случилось:

Большая крыса забралась в кухню,
Мы заткнули тряпкой дыру,
Которая служила крысе отступлением.
Несчастная крыса укрылась
Под угольный шкаф: ее оттуда выгоняют,
Но она исчезает.
Ищут, ищут во всех углах: крысы нет.
Утомившись войной,
Мы садимся играть в вист,
И тут горничная выходит,
Неся щипцами труп своего врага.
Вообразите себе, куда спряталась крыса:
В кухне стоял стул, а на этом стуле лежало платье горничной,
Крыса забралась в один из его рукавов.
Заметьте, что я трогал это платье
Четыре или пять раз
Во время наших поисков.

Не восхищаетесь ли Вы присутствием духа,
Быстротой глаза, энергией характера
Этого маленького животного?
Горничная уже собиралась уйти и оставить поиски,
Когда рукав чуть шевельнулся.

Бедная крыса заслуживала, чтобы спасти свою шкуру.
Вы привезете нам хорошую погоду.

IVAN TURGENEV TO PAULINE VIARDOT, A LETTER

Chateau de Courtavenel, Wednesday.
The other day was not as dull as the day before it.
We made a grand promenade,
and when we returned, a great event took place.
Here's what happened:

A large rat got into the kitchen,
we blocked its escape passage
with a rag. The poor rat
took cover under the corner cabinet:
we chase it out of there
and it vanishes.
We search and search all the corners: the rat is gone.
Exhausted by the warfare,
we sit down to a game of whist,
when a housemaid enters
carrying in the tongs her dead enemy.
Just imagine where the rat was hiding:
in the kitchen there was a chair, and on the chair hung the maid's dress,
the rat climbed into one of the sleeves.
Mind you, I touched that dress
four or five times
during our search.

Don't you admire the presence of mind,
the quickness of eye, the nerve and energy
of this small animal?
The housemaid was about to leave and stop the search
when the sleeve moved very slightly.

Poor rat deserved to be spared.
You will bring us good weather.

Мы не ждем Вас раньше субботы.
Ради Бога, берегите себя.

Tausend Grüsse

Не восхищаетесь ли Вы присутствием духа,
Быстротой глаза, энергией характера
Этого маленького животного
Ивана Тургенева,
Проведшего самый лакомый кус лета да и жизни всей
В ожидании той, которую раньше субботы
Ожидать не следует?

Его веселый писк,
Его вечерний вист,
Шуршанье, визг
Девочек в сыром красивом доме:
Луиза, Берта, Вероника.
Зевки и «скукота» и передергивание.

И где-то посреди него всего Полина
Ее зеленые слегка навыкате глаза
И голосы прямые смоляные
При легком смехе чуть дребезжащий голос
И узенький блестящий рыбий стан.

Был ли он в ней не был ли
Биографам понятно
Не вполне но
Она была в нем.
Она ходила в нем,
Ходила в нем, как в душной летней комнате Куртавенельской,

We do not expect you before Saturday.
I implore you, take care of yourself.

Tausend Grusse

Don't you admire the presence of mind,
the quickness of eye, the nerve and energy
of this small animal
known as Ivan Turgenev
who spent a sweet slice of summer and his life
expecting the one who before Saturday
shouldn't be expected?

His dolly squeak,
his daily whist,
the swish and shrieks
of girls in a rich damp house:
Louise, Berthe, Veronique.
Yawns and "ennui" and cheating at cards.

And someplace amid all that Pauline,
her green slightly bulgy eyes,
her hair, straight and jet-black,
her voice that, in the breeze of laughter, rattles a bit,
and a slender glistening of her fishlike frame.

Was he ever inside her or not
biographers know
not exactly but
she was inside him.
She walked inside him,
walked inside him as inside a sultry summer room at Courtavenel,

Покуда он
Лежал, отлично спрятавшись, и ждал
Разоблаченья:

Вот-вот найдет его
И будет шелка шум, и башмаков
И, как стрекозы, плоскеньких ее острот
Повсюду звон:

Он пошевелится, она его заметит наконец,
Она в брезгливости закружится, забьется,
А он заверещит:

Потоки поцелуев!
ВашВашВашВаш!

Ihr.

while he
waited well-hidden
to be discovered:

She is about to notice him.
The swish of silk and slippers
and the ringing of her flat jokes
like dragonflies from everywhere:

He will stir, she will finally notice this giant with a tiny voice.
She will twirl away squeamishly, cower,
and he would begin to squeal:

A gush of kisses!
YoursYoursYours!

Ihr.

КАТУЛЛ 68 (А) ЛИССАБОН

А.Д.

Я не знаю где ты мой брат
Возможно тебя нет более
Возможно тебя не было никогда.

Последнее, за что
Я держался или держалась к жизни
Была мысль, что далеко за морем
Брат мой, отвлекшись от меня
Поделывает что-то
Но теперь мне кажется
Что это я заврался.

Добрался до этого самого моря
Море обжигает меня.

Обжигает меня и город,
Где говорят его когда-то встречали
Люди, которым он говорил,
Что мог бы здесь задержаться на подольше
Что бы я сказал ему при встрече
Что бы мы стали делать
Что бы я ни сказал ему при встрече,
Возникла бы неловкость.
Я бы сразу сказал ему, что добился всего, чего искал
Скучающей брезгливости государя
Вожделения скучающей маленькой женщины
Видел как мои слова
Разошлись на граффити
В борделях, где мальчишки и девчонки
Выкрикали их картаво,
Кривляясь, почесываясь, и мочась
Он бы сказал, поморщившись:
И это что, все, что жизнь выжала из тебя?
Ради этого я возился с тобой, когда для всех

CATULLUS 68A LISBON

to A.D.

I don't know where these words will find you, brother.
It's possible that you are no longer,
it's possible that you have never been.
The last thing I held onto
in my life
was the thought that far beyond the sea
my brother, away from me,
is keeping busy
but now I wonder
whether it was a lie.
Now I've reached this sea,
the sea burns me.
The city too burns me.
Here, they say, people
met him, heard of his plans
to stay around longer.
What I would have told him,
what we would have done together,
nothing would have made our meeting
less awkward.
I would have told him that I've accomplished it all:
the yawning squeamishness of the monarch,
the lust of a bored little woman,
I saw my words
scratched on walls
of whorehouses where young boys and girls
burred them out
grimacing, itching, and pissing.
He would have made up a face:
is that all that life has squeezed out of you?
Is that what I bothered with you for

Ты был уродливым кукушонком?
То ли оранжевым, то ли синим, словно распухшим,
В руки такого не взять.
Ради вот этого я оставил тебя одного,
То есть обрек тебя тебе?
Я, бессловесный брат,—тебя, словесного брата?
Ну знаешь я бы ответил
Я знавал удовольствие, власть,
Когда раздвигаешь стих,
Как покорную женщину,
Так или эдак,
Как узкую улицу Альфамы,
Когда потом выходишь в орущую ночь
Пустой как младенец.—
Не ради удовольствия, но ради жалости
Я поставил на тебя,
Я рассчитывал, что ты научишься испытывать жалость
И научишься говорить об этом.
Жалость что слаще стыда и беспокойней любви,
Жалость что нас одна укрепляет в беседе на равных,
Жалость что щелочи злей омывает погнившую память
Жалость, которая нам позволяет ласкать и выгуливать мертвых,
Вдоль уязвленных волной йодом воняющих стен.
Тут я понял бы что
Умерший брат мой
Утратил ко мне интерес
Тень его перестала светиться
Он смотрит по сторонам
Вроде торопится
Или вспомнил пропажу
Вроде того что прощай

when others saw you as but an ugly runt?
Either orange or blue, as if bloated,
untouchable.
Is that what I left you alone for
sentencing you to yourself?
I, a wordless brother,—you, brother of many words?
Wait, I would have replied,
I've known the thrill of power
when you spread out your verse
like an eager woman
this way and that
like a narrow street in Alfama
and retreating later, blank like a newborn,
into the roaring night.
Yes, but I had expectations, not for the sake
of pleasure but mercy.
I thought you'd learn mercy,
learn its ways among words.
Mercy, sweeter than shame, mercy fidgety like love,
mercy that reaffirms us in the conversation of equals,
mercy that, like alkali, washes rotten memory,
mercy that allows us to caress and walk the dead
along the walls burnt by iodine waves.
Suddenly, I realized
that my dead brother
has lost interest,
his shadow no longer shines,
his eyes wonder,
he seems in a rush
or has remembered something he lost,
something like a goodbye.

POTTERY/POETRY

Ремесло, которое выбрала я, и ремесло, которое выбрало меня,
Причудливо соотносятся... Если бы! В самом деле...
Слова расползаются, как подушка и простыня
В битве бессонницы. Глина растёт, как опухоль на невинном теле.
Поэзия ржавой ложкой снимает пенки, сливки, навар, дородный слой
С жижицы недоуменья, скопившегося за сутки.
Глина же соучаствует в каждом акте, берёт на себя мою ответственность передо мной,
Держится до последнего содроганья иглы, мастерка и губки.
И главное — всё это молча. С той мощной немотой,
Что исключает возможность не только диа-, но главное — монолога.
Поэтому от разыскивающей меня Этой всё чаще я прячусь в Той
И вслушиваюсь злорадно в тяжёлую поступь Бога:
Он ищет меня по улицам Питера. Днём — с огнём,
А белой ночью — с собаками: Достоевским, Гоголем, со спаниелем-Блоком.
А я сижу, вжимаясь в стенку кувшина, притворяюсь вином
И надеюсь на то, что в горлышко властным оком
Он не вопьётся, не различит на дне
Беглую прораб(ыню) с его галеры,
Потому что когда Он всё же подносит губы свои ко мне,
Я различаю сквозь запах уксуса запах серы.
И не то чтоб сей образный ряд возбуждал во мне резкий звук
Выбора, отвращенья, беды, морали,
Но если (привет М. Б.!) есть Верх и Низ, то мне бы хотелось дожить внизу
Жизнь, которую у меня... — у которой меня украли.
И не то чтоб кого-то хотелось мне обвинять
(Ведь объект и субъект едины у обвиненья),
Но глина, жалеющая меня, и поэзия, пожирающая меня,
Есть две вещи, не совместимые с точки зрения зренья.

POTTERY/POETRY

The craft I have picked and the craft that has picked me
are amusingly related... If only! In reality...
Words dishevel like sheets and pillows
in the battle of insomnia. The clay grows like a tumor on innocent flesh.
With a rusty spoon, poetry takes the foam / cream / fat, and
    fertile topsoil
off the brew of bewilderment amassed over a day.
Clay co-touches, takes charge of my responsibility for myself,
endures till the last spasm of the needle / float / sponge.
All is performed in silence. In that great silence
that excludes a possibility of not only dialog but, most
    importantly, monolog.
This is why from this *Po* chasing me, I more and more often hide
    inside that *Po*
and I listen attentively spitefully to God's heavy footsteps:
He is chasing me on the streets of P. In the day—with pale fire,
in the white night—with hounds: Dostoyevsky, Gogol, and Blok
    the spaniel.
While I, like a drop of wine, press myself to the side of a jug
hoping that His possessive eye won't peek
into the spout, won't spy
on its bottom His runaway serf.
When He nears his lips towards me,
in the smell of vinegar, I discern the smell of sulfur.
And it's not that this alchemy strikes in me a high sound
of choice, disgust, misery, virtue,
but if Bakhtin's carnivalesque is right and there is High and Low,
    then I'd prefer the life of low Po
that was stolen from me—from which I was stolen.
And it's not that I want to accuse anybody
(the subject and the object of this accusation are one),
but this clay that takes pity on me, and this poetry that devours me
are incompatible from the point of view of viewing.

«Зрение» — так называется последний приют таких
Нечестивиц, как я, лишивших себя иного.
Глаз раскрывает поверхность, палец пронзает стих,
Стенки сосуда рушатся, чувствуя натиск Слова.

Sight is the last refuge of such
unfortunates as myself who have deprived themselves of the rest.
An eye opens the surface, a finger rips through a poem,
the walls of the vessel collapse under the pressure of Word.

AFTERWORD & COMMENTARY

INTERNATIONAL DAY OF SIRENS:
A CONVERSATION IN LIEU OF AN AFTERWORD

Valzhyna: The Siege of Leningrad began in 1941 and lasted 872 days, resulting in the most destructive blockade in history. Leningrad, already shaken by the Stalinist purges of the 1930s, withstood at great human cost. The lives that ended in the '30s and '40s border on indefinite vanishing. Many biographies give a date of birth along with a date of a posthumous "rehabilitation," but no date of death. Or, otherwise, they have a date of birth and an approximate period of vanishing: some last sightings mentioned in the diaries of similarly vanished ghosts.

No public language was developed for talking about either the events of the Soviet terror or the Siege; there is no public verbal memory. Placeholders like "you know... you understand" or "well... yeah" mark the threshold of the non-verbalized facts of arrests, kidnappings, persecution, executions, banishments into labor camps, starvation, and abandonment to slow death. What kind of language comes after the end of a catastrophe? How does language respond to terror?

In this situation of a great lack of language, you describe your work in the archives as the descent of locusts devouring everything in their path: diaries, letters, memoirs. You emerged out of these verbose, passionate, emotional accounts of personal terror straight into the public discourse determined by those who inflicted terror. It is an environment fertile for poetry: simultaneously overflowing with language and lacking it. The same is true, though in different circumstances, for translation: there is an arsenal of possibilities, yet no real equivalence; simultaneous lack and abundance.

What is the Leningrad of your childhood? What is the Leningrad of the archives? Where do these two Leningrads— one lived and the other read/researched, one of a poet and the other of a scholar—meet?

Polina: When I was six years old my parents took me to the opening ceremony of the huge monument dedicated to the Siege of Leningrad—I remember its magnitude, and granite, and golden letters everywhere—that was overwhelming and completely strange, foreign, not about me. And then my parents showed me a piece of tiny black matter—a piece of the "bread" (made of something completely inedible) that was rationed in the city during the winter of 1941-1942.

And I still remember the taste of tears in my throat when I saw it: this bread looked like coal, like something from Hell. It is this memory that returns to me and that I return to when I have to explain my first "encounter" with the Siege.

This question—where is besieged Leningrad for me now— is so complicated, so big, so layered: yes, indeed, it's in the archives, in the diaries. It's in the artworks and poetry.

Yet also, in that city, it's virtually everywhere, in ghostly form. For example, I spent my childhood in a little park called "Victory Park": little did we know that during the Siege that whole place was an improvised "cemetery" (meaning a ravine with emaciated dead bodies) and a crematorium. So, we played there, flirted there, right "above" the ashes of those people, those children—and nobody told us. The improvised graveyard was our playground. Of course, it's horrific, but now I think about it as a meeting place: here we were silently together with the Siege ghosts.

People who research various genocides tell us that trauma produces emptiness and silence, muteness. The Siege overflowed with texts. It produced verbal diarrhea. Among them, texts of the highest quality, most amazing insight, intellect, observation. The Siege had Lydia Ginzburg and Gennady Gor the way the camps had Paul Celan. Gennady Gor produced a language the size and shape of horror, or lament.

Valzhyna: A few days ago, you sent me a postcard congratulating me with the international day of sirens. In Russian, a siren is a mythological bird-fish-woman who lures sailors with her unfathomable singing, but a siren is also a word for an air raid warning, an alarm. Here we are in your city of sailors and sirens. Here it is: a huge granite monument where speeches are delivered and flowers are placed. Simultaneously, in the same city, there exists a coal-like, hell-like piece of bread. Words said over this bread were different from the words said by the monument. Lives stopped or continued for an extra day because of this piece of bread. There it is, like a hidden, magical object that the hero in a fairy tale must search out, a frightening treasure.

I'm glad you brought up Lydia Ginzburg. Ginzburg's *Blockade Diary* records life in Leningrad under the Siege. It's 1941. There are daily bombardments, starvation, freezing temperatures, no heating or electricity in the ruins where people fall asleep and wake up to the sound of the loudspeaker alerting the remaining citizens of air raids and reciting speeches of encouragement. Ginzburg describes this voice from the loudspeakers as human, yet unnatural; a voice interrupted by technical glitches. "The voice spoke unnaturally slowly," she writes.

Isn't that a definition of a poetic voice? Slow, focused on articulation (our parents teach us to chew slowly while poets teach us to slow down our speech, to articulate, to think-speak); a voice interrupted by rusty glitches in the mechanism of language that resists uncommon usages and turns.

Unnatural, yet human, this voice resides in the air, speaking to whomever would listen.

Polina: I do remember when I began reading, reciting poetry like that—it was in a Young Pioneer camp called "Young Children of Felix Dzerzhinsky" [the first leader of the Soviet secret police]. My parents sent me there every June. Predictably, this was a very ideologically correct and robust Pioneer camp and we, the children, had to play our roles. I chose to read poetry out loud at camp meetings. I was given some poems about the atrocities of capitalism and Soviet victims of all possible wars. I had to memorize them and then to perform them—and I remember that I chose to read them out very loudly and very, very slowly, to everybody's shock. Yet, it worked—there was total silence and some unpleasant attention, I knew I had that crowd. Once a girl asked me, "Why do you recite so slowly?" And I said, "But it is very difficult poetry, very difficult words, they cannot be rushed."

I still hold in my mind that sound and that image of a recital of a poem about a massacre in a silence that is of my making. God knows what would have become of me and my voice/power/pleasures if the Soviet Union hadn't collapsed. Anyhow, what stayed with me was this feeling that the voice is a very flexible and a very treacherous thing. In one of my poems, called "Voice" I recreate the situation of the "Siege Muse," poet Olga Bergholz, who worked with Ginzburg at the radio by the way, and who was absolutely taken by this sensation that she could bring some sort of vitality to the "dead" apartments with her voice alone. She had no bread, no heat to give—only something so useless, yet so comforting as poetry.

What has translation to offer in relation to this fragile, enchanting power? First and foremost, I am interested in the collaboration of translation because for me translation is the most intimate and the most intense effort of interpretation possible.

Rarely do you meet a reader whom you can ask to read your work obsessively—it is normal to skip, to jump through pages, to be frivolous, but a translator, a real translator, doesn't have this freedom, this joy of non-commitment and laziness. So, a poet meets his/her utmost reader and this reader can be very unpleasant—because he/she sees it all, up-close. In our process, you constantly asked me all kinds of questions—like a detective or a jealous lover: "Why did you choose this word? This sound? This figure?" It makes one revisit one's choices—like revisiting the scene of crime: it is totally fascinating.

Valzhyna: And like in a good detective story, it's never the words you suspect would give you the most trouble that end up rogue. It's those plain, always-around words, like "laughter" or "yellow" that make me suspicious because poetic speech strangifies them, imbuing them with tension and power usually not given to such plain words.

Plain Russian words seep into my English not to foreignize the text, but to emphasize that these poems are invested in the power of language and voice, in the question of who gets to speak and be heard and how it happens. The original Russian is strange and disruptive to the native reader just as it is disruptive to the English reader. What can be read as my "liberties" and "creative license," to me are moments of most semantic fidelity to the freedom and creativity of your poems. I wonder, Polina, do you have an idea about how you'd like to be translated?

Polina: Actually, my main requirement, and mostly for myself, rather than for my translator, is that of freedom—I need to feel that we are free in this process, that the translator has their unique, idiosyncratic relationship with my text. Starting from my collaboration with Ilya Kaminsky, who translated my first American book, I understood that I really enjoy the translator having a happy affair with my text, passionate and individualistic. Each translator will see in my text what they need; and, hopefully, I can learn something from their vision, from their understanding.

For example, in your translation, "Sunny Morning in the Square" at the end, rather than my somewhat awkward line "when you die, let me know, I'll follow you there…" you begin a horrific beautiful game of sounds—which I had left underdeveloped. Your ending sounds like the howling of greyhounds, the noise of guns, the screams of people in the square—I really like it. I believe that in the case of our collaboration here, you sometimes develop what you, as a reader, see as essential for this text—and this becomes transplanted into a new language, into your language. It's a new, other life of this poem. I am not that interested in translations being exact replicas, pale simulacra; I want, ideally, translations of my poems to be wild.

Valzhyna: "A Sunny Morning in the Square," a poem about the deportation of Jews from the town of Białystok, opens with a train "padded in fright like a Christmas star" and ends with the image of this star cracking: "you crack like a glass Christmas star. Arrr arrr" This hard German "r" that falls off the cracked "star" enacts in English something that is indeed not in the original Russian. And yet, it is there, perhaps not exactly in this place, not exactly like that. Earlier in the poem, the citizens of Białystok read an announcement that starts off very formally: "You are to appear in person on the square at six." But already with the second line, something is off: "bring only your wrist watches, in the amount of twelve." The formal quality of the pronouncement is made strange with this exact (and large!) amount of personal watches, that are the "only" thing allowed. By the last line of the pronouncement, what seemed direct and formal, is just bizarre: "bring only one bolt and one hatch." This packing is unnatural and the mouth making pronouncements—the mouth speaking from the mouth of a poet—is enacting this unnaturalness by slowly breaking. The ending represents the final breakage.

Both English and Russian are imperial languages systematically used to justify violence. This commonality makes the breaking translatable, particularly by a translator like me, for whom Russian is a stepmother tongue, an imposed, colonial language. When I translate your work, I get to break Russian while wearing the gloves of English—I'm an untraceable Belarusian criminal.

As a poet and a translator, I'm in a rather unique situation: I write in two languages, Belarusian and English, neither of which is my "mother-tongue." The longer I've lived and worked in this linguistic triangle of English, Belarusian, and Russian, the blurrier the walls between languages appear to be. I think of all of my linguistic matter as one language. My faithfulness is to the pitch that turns a human voice into the voice of a siren. In practice, it means dedication to the tension between poetic elements, to the degree of the grotesque, to the sharpness of turns and leaps of association. As for words and meanings, they always take care of themselves in the end.

So you see, my relationship with my three languages is that of trust. I trust that a language will provide. In some cultures, they say that a newborn brings a loaf of bread to feed itself with. I believe that certain poems bring their own translation with them, in the crook of their arm. I have to hear it, with my intuitive, musical ear.

Translation of poetry is above all intuitive: we repeat so as not to forget. Once we get into this habit of repeating in another language, the translation of poetry becomes a moral habit. We translate because we refuse to forget.

In the third part of the "Hampshire College Archive" cycle, you draw out of the oblivion of the Warsaw Ghetto the name of a toddler, Margalit. In a note that miraculously survives, thus turning into a testimony, the father praises his twenty-month-old child for being able to acquire speech fast and early: "Margalit gavalit" (in English, "Margalit speaks," or, in my translation, "Margalit sp-hics"). You turned what should have been "*govorit*" into "*gavalit*": the hard "*r*" in "*govorit*" is softened into "*l*" ("*gavalit*"), while the vowels in the unstressed position turn from "o" into "a." This vowel shift, together with the soft "l," indicate a child's manner of speaking. Margalit cannot yet properly pronounce the word for "[he/she/it] speaks" but she already rhymes this verb with her name (Marga*lit*—gava*lit*).

To create a similar playfulness in English, I imagine a hiccupping child—hiccupping after breastfeeding—which is why instead of being unable to pronounce the hard Russian "r," in English, Margalit hiccups through speech—she "sp-hics": half-speech, half-spasm. In Russian and English, the "lit" in the rhyming pair of "Marga*lit*—gava*lit*" accidentally conjures "literature." Margalit speaks through your poem. Margalit isn't in oblivion, she is in literature.

Curiously, the hard German "arrr" from "A Sunny Morning in the Square" is exactly what little Margalit cannot pronounce in the Russian word for "speaks." The hard "r" is also the letter that separates her name from Paul Celan's Margarete in "Death Fugue," who is also Goethe's Margarete. Therefore, in English, this "arrr" and "Margalit" are two pieces of a frightening puzzle.

Earlier in the poem, there's a half-mention of Margalit's mother: "(whose name here is meaningless, / leave her be now nameless and faceless)." Like this: in parenthesis, in the margins of the narrative there remains a name we never learn.

In "A Passionate Damsel, or the Exploits of Zinaida C." you open an archival folder of Zinaida Bykova, a talentless translator of French symbolism, aided by her more successful husband, but eaten alive by the critics nonetheless. What makes Zina's story so heartbreaking is that the war arrives, the Siege arrives, and she vanishes. We can imagine Zina's tragic death; we have to imagine the worst. Her death in the Siege turns all these facts of her life inside out: her poor translations full of mistakes, her husband's generous favors, the mocking reviews of her work, her naïve desire to belong to the literary world. All of this is redeemed by her invisible death, isn't it?

A bad writer and translator who didn't bother to look up words in the dictionary is now my muse. Working on your poems, I asked for guidance not from St. Jerome, the patron saint of translators, but from Zinaida Bykova, a failed translator.

Polina: I think you are touching here upon a very important question: for whom—that is, on whose behalf—do we speak? We know (that is, we were taught) that literature is nothing but a dialogue—continuing through time. And, allegedly, we can choose our interlocutors. What interests me, perhaps, are interlocutors having speech troubles. A million *blokadniki*— the inhabitants (including dozens of poets) of besieged, starving Leningrad, the city where I grew up. In spite of all our efforts, we'll never hear from most of them, they are traceless in history, voiceless. And something really upsets me about that, really troubles me—and makes me write. That was the case with Zinaida Bykova, the hack translator who disappeared in the snow drifts of the dying city: this very word "disappeared" fills me with anger towards history and tenderness towards her. Yet, obviously, it's not only about the tragedy of the Siege. The disappearance of Catullus, or, differently, of Pushkin or Chekhov also ignites some reaction of writing—Chekhov spent his last years coughing up blood, with his voice completely changed. Because of TB, he looked like an old man at 42, and he already knew that he'd never write that novel of his. It might be a delusion, it might be a grave moral mistake, but I feel that sometimes poets can spare some words to the dead.

Auden said, "poetry makes nothing happen," and we've been wondering ever since—are we so impotent, so powerless? Poetry cannot shoot, cannot heal, cannot abolish death. Poetry's jobs are minor: to comfort a mourner, a lover, for a brief moment. Elegy, one of the earliest forms of poetry, was born as funeral song. As I see it now, the job of consolation is crucial, the job of giving medicine—even if it cannot bring anybody back to life, it can patch the texture of life as it is, make it softer, warmer. Damn it, make it prettier.

Valzhyna: A funeral song is no longer only for a funeral. We need a funeral song for a children's playground built over a site of mass executions. We need funeral songs for the ghosts of our cities—people disappeared into history without a funeral. Poetry does make conversations happen, between the living and the dead. Could you say more about the presence of other writers in this book? Some of them appear as characters in your poems, others appear as co-authors, others are the addressees, and others have poems dedicated to them.

There's so much writing and reading happening in this book: from a note on a piece of paper hidden in a tin to the love letters of Russian nineteenth-century classic Ivan Turgenev; from the letters of the non-literary Miller family to a poem that reads as a musical with twentieth-century Russian writers as performers (Zinaida Gippius, Daniil Kharms, Samuil Marshak, Elena Guro). There's also Charles Dickens, Emily Dickinson, Catullus... Contemporary writers and scholars that appear are Sergei Dovlatov, Aleksandr Skidan, Ilya Kaminsky, Irina Sandomirskaya. What is the relationship between the nameless notes/letters and the beloved published authors?

Among all of these co-authors and interlocutors, there's one that stands out to me: Shahrazad [Scheherazade] and other references to *The Arabian Nights* (Mutabor, Caliph Stork, Aladdin). What is the significance of this ancient storyteller? Who is Caliph Stork (utterly unknown to an American reader) to you? I know that, unlike in the US, *The Arabian Nights* was very popular in the Soviet Union. Is it a formative text for you?

Polina: I also noticed recently that there are more and more dedications in my poems. This turns into a symptom, and into a device: my poems become letters. I can think of many explanations for this, trivial ones—the eternal quest for a (perfect) reader, erotic courtship and gift making—but also I began thinking that the poem is a ritual for me. Many of my poems, most of my poems concern death. Talking about death in polite society is awkward—but if you do it in the form of a poem, chances are people will accept your awkward and embarrassing utterance. So, by addressing people in poems I help them to accept my speech.

What really was formative was a Russian rewrite of *The Arabian Nights* and the fairy tales of the early-nineteenth-century poet Wilhelm Hauff, who died at 25 and yet managed to produce some of the scariest, most mysterious, most poignant stories I know—they speak to me in many tiny, scary, beautiful tongues. In general, I find fairy tales very useful, with their shocking, weird versions of femininity—like Baba Yaga, for example, who exists beyond gender, beyond age, perhaps even beyond biological species limitations. Baba Yaga, who is able to make love to the Prince and to eat him during the same dinner, so to speak. The same goes for Shahrazad: she is so touching but also somewhat scary, with her stubborn desire to avert peril by any means: by love-making, by story-telling. This version of the poet is very dear to me: you think that as long as you are weaving your story, as long as somebody is listening, you are saved—and you can save others—from death.

The title of the cycle "Mutabor" also comes from Hauff's pseudo-Arabian fairy tale about a prince who turns into a bird, a stork, and has to stay a bird because he forgets a magic word—"mutabor." This fairy tale struck me as a child with its total desire for a magic word that would give us power and which makes us its slaves, its servants. For me, this story about the power, even the danger, of the magic word is symbolic of our craft in general: we use very strong material and sometimes I feel our words have control over us, not the other way around. At some point I wanted to call this whole book *Mutabor* instead of *Air Raid*. Of course, it's so strange, it is a non-word, very trans-sense. That is what attracted the poor stork-prince and what attracted me. And also the whole play of laughter and forgetting: the prince forgets the magic word because he laughs—through laughter he loses his humanity. I think it's such a charged, scary text—it can engender many poems!

Valzhyna: What if it were not death that Shahrazad was afraid of? What if Shahrazad were afraid of being Zinaida C.—afraid that she is not a good poet? She is afraid that her throat will be cut before she tells her best story.

In your poem "A Guide to Leningrad Writers, Veterans 1941–1945," we hear a polyphony of poetic voices. It's a long poem that appears very theatrical, where the fantastic of fairy tales is mixed with the fantastic (absurd, unreal, unbelievable) of history. Its six parts are acts of a frightening musical. In the very first line, Masha's brains get mashed, Kharms gets drunk, and ration cards—the sole guarantee of survival under the Siege—go missing. What follows is the hysterical empty-ing of one's bag, brains, stomach, in search of this ration card that guarantees one more day of life. The emptying is total: all of the previously absorbed cultural heritage from Russian folk ballads to foreign literature, the high and the low of language, fact and gossip, murder and dance, are vomited in six goes. I use Russian words in this poem: Russian falls out of English during uncontrollable spasms. "Darling" turns into "DA-DA-DA-darling"; Leningrad citizens are intertwined with apparat-chiks, producing "Leningradtchiks." Like many of your poems, this one does not end with any logical resolution. Its ending only comes when the loudspeaker is broken—it goes on and on until the poem breaks.

Polina: That is a very tricky, packed question—how should one read this complicated poetry, packed with names, events, allusions often unknown to the Western reader, moreover, un-known even to the post-Soviet user of the Soviet culture.

I think there are several ways to approach this task: one is that of meticulous scholarly research, indeed following the clues one finds in these poems, one can study the Siege—as I once chose to study it—and this exploration still has so many gaps, so many "black holes." This text indeed is a provocation to know more, but even more so it is a provocation to feel, to be empathic. I think that on some level it is enough for a reader to know that there was, in the twentieth century, this city of Leningrad and that it suffered an awful kind of suffering—of hungry death. And in that troubled city, there lived poets who attempted to find words for this ordeal.

"A Guide to Leningrad Writers, Veterans 1941–1945" is a text just about that—poets in the city of death, their feelings, their instruments, like voice or hearing or imaginary flight, the de-sire to escape. I see that my task in conversation with you, my translator, is to give to my reader various clues to come into contact with these texts: for those who need knowledge there are commentaries, for those who enter a poem as an emotional experience and possibility—there are images, sounds, shadows, and memories. Indeed, I want the whole world to know more about the Siege, because I cannot bear that all those people would be forgotten in the dark snow. But also there's a paradox here, since some of it just cannot be known, cannot be comprehended. We will never know what happened to Zinaida C.—not just her death, but also her life was devoured by history.

When we speak about the Siege today, we often remember great artists who wrote about it—Dmitri Shostakovich with his Symphony No. 7, for example—but we do not talk about the less famous, the less fortunate—like Matiushina (O.M., as she appears in the cycle) or Panteleev (L.P.) or Krandievskaia (N.K.), those who didn't write grand works about the Siege using the grand support of the grand state. My work combines loud voices, widely heard voices with those who did not find much support, who did not make it into the Siege canon. And I hope that some of my questions are not only local, specific for the Siege of Leningrad, but global—how do we remember many fractured, invisible lives disappeared by disaster, sometimes even without a trace? Do we forget them, just leave them there or do we voice them, and how?

My utmost intention, my hope, is that the reader will feel as strongly for the unfortunate poetess Zinaida C.—or for the helpless people who come in horror to the square on any summer morning where people in uniforms await them—as for the titans and heroes of history. To me, Zinaida and her disappearance is as important as Shostakovich, who, by the way, was airlifted in September 1941 so that he could write about the Siege for the whole world. My main provocation in these poems has to do with the fact that we often allow ourselves to imagine that we really know history—though there is so much, especially in history's wounds, that is almost impossible or at least very difficult to know. Perhaps I write about this bitter temptation to fight the offenses of history with knowledge and also with the acceptance that sometimes knowledge is not possible, that we need imagination and compassion.

Valzhyna: Allow me then to appear now, like Ole Lukøje (from Hans Christian Andersen's story), with an umbrella under my arm. When I open my umbrella and spin it in front of our readers, they will fall asleep and see strange, scary dreams. In these dreams, they will lose sight of what is real and what is fantasy, what is living and what is dead. Here they are on a train to Białystok ("A Sunny Morning in the Square"); there we are on a bus to Auschwitz ("Auschwitz-Birkenau, a Guided Tour for American Students"). "What year is it?" they wonder, "brushing Marlboro ashes / on the ashes made here, shed here." In this ambiguous smoke, the Virgil driving the train/bus is lost, circling the twentieth century, from the "Auschwitz" of Białystok to Auschwitz, in search of words.

Time and borders spin and our moment merges with 1939 (the year the Soviets occupied Białystok) and with 1941 (the year of the Nazi occupation). The town reflects our arrival in the distorted mirror of history: we arrive as the citizens of Białystok are told to pack and prepare for departure. Are they leaving on the train we've arrived on? Could it be that our dream train is also a death train?

We are lost in time because time is New Year's Eve, the night of a magical time shift. The whole town is being packed "like a Christmas star," a fragile topping of private gatherings glittering in the dark. (It's New Year's, not Christmas, that is celebrated in the opening poem, as is traditional in Eastern

Europe). This family heirloom—a fragile star of private lives—is countered with the stars of public narratives: the Soviet star, the star of David, and the swastika that shines, star-like, on the forehead of a German officer overseeing the timely departures on the train of death. The private lives are gone: either crushed or sealed away from the public eye. While Western discourse has serialized and overproduced the narratives of twentieth century pain, the Russian (and Soviet) discourse has done everything not to allow such an archive to exist.

The many poems that follow hand us the honor and shame of unsealing the private spaces padded from the catastrophic shaking of their epoch. We will enter apartments of the dead, led by an unlikely team of Virgils—librarians and policemen—in order to unpack them, like time capsules. We will unseal private letters, examine the walls of torture chambers. With a finger, we will go through the layers of thawing corpses seeking an encounter with one dear corpse. Why this obsession with the dead? A Russian poet cannot part with the dead of the twentieth century because she has never properly encountered them.

These poems are *en route*, to use Paul Celan's phrase. Their destination: an encounter. We have to greet each other—the living and the dead—in order to be able to say goodbye.

The poet is readying herself for this encounter by collecting the magical, otherworldly words that have power to protect and to charm, like gems. In the world of breaking Christmas stars and forgotten private lives, gems endure. In a poetics built on breakage, gems are unbreakable. An earring is found ("Joy") in order to whisper into the poet's ear. Also, a note from a concentration camp with Margalit's name written in it. The toddler is the age of the poet's own daughter. A sign? For the obsessed, signs shimmer from everywhere: pearls turn into sugar, sugar turns into ice, ice turns into Leningrad, Leningrad spills into mouths hungry for food and words. In these poems full of eroticism, a mouth good at loving often fails at words, collapsing into a mute handful of pearly teeth. Such poetic transactions teach me how to translate these poems. I hardly notice how this happens—translation of poetry is a kind of a dream. I lose a sense of whether your poems have already been written or not, and I write them again, in a language not mine.

For a poem that seeks an encounter with an obsessed Other, its encounter with a translator—the most obsessive kind of reader—is the ultimate encounter. Like poetry, translation of poetry is not the means. Translation of poetry is an encounter of two obsessed souls. I do not look for words I can attach on top of other words. Quite to the contrary, translation of poetry in this book is about releasing words back into their freedom. "Circling around a thing is a free word, like the soul of an abandoned but not forgotten body," writes Osip Mandelstam in 1921. "A word is a Psyche," he writes. Also, a word is a siren, another winged being.

Poetry translation is akin to stargazing or birdwatching: deep listening in the thicket of language. There is no intention of capture here, only attention to what is free. I could go further and say that translating these poems is like Psyche-gazing, like siren-watching. "There was neither a hero nor a poet on Odysseus's ship," Marina Tsvetaeva writes. "A hero would withstand without being tied, without wax in her ears. A poet would jump overboard even when tied, a poet would hear even with wax in her ears."

NOTES TO THE POEMS

CHILDEN'S LITERATURE

This poem refers to several Leningrad poets and writers connected to the circle of the OBERIU (Union of Real Art; one of the last Soviet avant-garde groupings) who also wrote literature for children and worked in children's book and magazine publishing: Daniil Kharms, Evgeny Shvarts, Nikolai Oleinikov, Aleksandr Vvedensky, Konstantin Vaginov.

"AFTER THE WAR HE FOUND HIMSELF IN THE WEST"

Old Lady Gippius — Zinaida Gippius (1869–1945), poet, diarist, who emigrated to Paris after the revolutions of 1917. At the beginning of WWII, Gippius expressed solidarity with the Nazis on account of their anti-Bolshevik ideas.

AN ENCOUNTER

epigraph — Nikolai Nikulin (1923-2009) was an art historian and author of a memoir about World War II.

AIR RAID

The letters that inspired this text were written by the Miller-Tatarovich family, which consisted of Nikolai Miller, the father, Maria Miller, the grandmother, and Irina (Tata) Miller, Nikolai's young daughter. Nikolai was arrested and sent to the Gulag (forced-labor camps) and Tata wrote to him while being evacuated from the besieged Leningrad to the Siberian village of Emurtla, where the grandmother chose to remain and perished from hunger in July 1942.

A GUIDE TO LENINGRAD WRITERS, VETERANS 1941-1945

L.P. — Leonid Panteleev (1908-1987) was a renowned Soviet writer of literature for children. He worked for the same state publishing house as many of the OBERIU-related writers mentioned in the poem "Children's Literature" (see note above).

Kharms — Daniil Ivanovich Iuvachev (1905-1942), pen name Kharms, was the leader of the avant-garde poetry association OBERIU and a writer and translator of children's literature. Kharms was arrested in Leningrad in August 1941 for alleged "pro-German sympathizing." Upon psychiatric examination, he was incarcerated in the psychiatric ward of the infamous "Crosses" (Kresty) prison, where he died of malnutrition during the most severe period of the Leningrad Siege famine.

O.B. — Olga Berggolts (1910-1975), a Leningrad poet, was imprisoned for several months in 1939. In 1941, during the Siege of Leningrad, she chose not to leave the city, unlike Akhmatova and other writers. She worked for the Leningrad radio through the whole duration of the Siege.

Radio Bureau — the radio committee where many Leningrad writers worked during the Siege was located on Rakova Street.

O.M. — Olga Matiushina (1885-1975), widow of the avant-garde composer and visual artist Mikhail Matiushin. She lost her sight during one of the Siege bombings. She later wrote a memoir about her Siege experience.

V.V. — Vsevolod Vishnevsky (1900-1951), one of the leaders of the Leningrad Soviet Writers Union during the Siege.

Mikhail Vasilievch — Composer and artist Mikhail Matiushin (1861-1934) was a key member of several Petersburg Futurist groups before the revolution and was active in Soviet avant-garde circles of the 1920s. His close friends included painter Kazimir Malevich and poet Velemir Khlebnikov. His first wife was the writer and artist Elena Guro.

Elena Genrikhovna / Guro — Elena Guro (1877–1913), a central figure of the early Russian avant-garde, was an influential poet and artist that belonged to Petersburg Futurist circles.

N.K. — Natalia Krandievskaia (1888–1963), a poet.

Suvorin —Alexei Suvorin (1834–1912), a publisher and editor.

V.I. — Vera Inber (1890–1972), poet and diarist. In 1946, she received the Stalin Prize for her Siege poetry.

JOY

Polina Annenkova — a seamstress from Paris who followed her husband, Ivan Annenkov, one the participants of the Decembrist revolt in Petersburg (1825), into exile in Siberia.

HAMPSHIRE COLLEGE ARCHIVE

Israel Lichtenstein — together with Emanuel Ringelblum, one of the creators of the Oyneg Shabes Archive (1942–1944), a collection of testimonies, documents, newspapers, diaries, photographs, and artworks related to the Warsaw Ghetto and the Jewish resistence.

MUTABOR

M. Semenko — Mikhal Semenko (1892–1937) is perhaps the best known of the Ukrainian Futurist poets.

Alexander S. — Aleksandr Skidan, contemporary Petersburg poet and literary critic.

ROMANTIC WALKS THROUGH CITY CEMETERIES

Sergei Dovlatov (1941–1990) — Leningrad prose writer and journalist who emigrated to New York City in 1979.

FAMILY FLIGHT TO EGYPT

Sergei Parajanov (1924–1990) — a Soviet filmmaker, screenwriter, and artist of Armenian and Ukranian descent. Most of his film projects from 1965 to 1973 were banned or blocked by the Soviet film administrations. He was arrested on defamatory charges including homosexuality in 1973. After his release in 1977, he continued to face harassment by the authorities until the mid-1980s, when he was finally able to resume making films.

IVAN TURGENEV TO PAULINE VIARDOT, A LETTER

Ivan Turgenev (1818–1883) — one of the most important Russian novelists of the nineteenth-century, author of *Fathers and Sons*.

Polina Viardot (1821–1910) — a renowned French opera singer and the romantic partner of Russian novelist Ivan Turgenev, who followed her to France.

ACKNOWLEDGEMENTS

The translator wishes to gratefully acknowledge that work on this book was supported by a National Endowment for the Arts Literature Fellowship and a grant from the New York State Council on the Arts. Some of the translated poems in this collection first appeared in *Modern Poetry in Translation*, *Ambit*, *Gulf Coast Journal*, *Washington Square Review*, and *Bennington Review* —our gratitude to the editors of these journals. The poem "Air Raid" recieved a Gulf Coast Translation Prize. Many thanks to Matvei Yankelevich and Elina Alter for their editorial suggestions and careful proofreading.

ABOUT THE AUTHOR

Polina Barskova is a poet and a scholar, author of twelve collections of poems and two books of prose in Russian. Her collection of creative nonfiction, *Living Pictures*, received the Andrey Bely Prize in 2015 and is forthcoming in German with Suhrkamp Verlag and in English with NYRB. She is the editor of *Written in the Dark: Five Poets in the Siege of Leningrad* (Ugly Duckling Presse) and has three collections of poetry published in English translation: *This Lamentable City* (Tupelo Press), *The Zoo in Winter* (Melville House) and *Relocations* (Zephyr Press). She has taught at Hampshire College, Amherst College, and Smith College. She teaches Russian Literature at the University of California at Berkeley.

ABOUT THE TRANSLATOR

Valzhyna Mort was born in Minsk, Belarus. She is the author of the poetry collections *Factory of Tears*, *Collected Body* (both from Copper Canyon Press), and *Music for the Dead and Resurrected* (FSG), which was shortlisted for the International Griffin Prize and named one of the best poetry book of 2020 by *The New York Times*. Mort is a recipient of an NEA Literature Fellowship (for translation), as well as fellowships from the American Academy in Rome and the Lannan Foundation. Her work has been honored with the Bess Hokin Prize from *Poetry*, the Glenna Luschei *Prairie Schooner* Award, and was shortlisted for the Forward Prize. She teaches at Cornell University and writes in English and Belarusian.

The Eastern European Poets Series from Ugly Duckling Presse

0   *The Gray Notebook*
    Alexander Vvedensky

1   *Attention and Man*
    Ilya Bernstein

2   *Calendar*
    Genya Turovskaya

3   *Poker*
    Tomaž Šalamun

4   *Fifty Drops of Blood*
    Dmitri Prigov

5   *Catalogue of Comedic Novelties*
    Lev Rubinstein

6   *The Blue Notebook*
    Daniil Kharms

7   *Sun on a Knee*
    Tone Škrjanec

8   *Less Than a Meter*
    Mikhail Aizenberg

9   *Chinese Sun*
    Arkadii Dragomoshchenko

10 *Iterature*
    Eugene Ostashevsky

11 *The Song of Igor's Campaign*
    Bill Johnston, tr.

12 *Do Not Awaken Them
    With Hammers*
    Lidija Dimkovska

13 *New Translations*
    Osip Mandelstam

14 *Paper Children*
    Mariana Marin

15 *The Drug of Art*
    Ivan Blatný

16 *Red Shifting*
    Alexander Skidan

17 *As It Turned Out*
    Dmitri Golynko

18 *The Russian Version*
    Elena Fanailova

19 *Dreaming Escape*
    Valentina SaraÇini

20 *Poker* [2nd Ed.]
    Tomaž Šalamun

21 *Sun on a Knee* [2nd Ed.]
    Tone Škrjanec

22 *Slovene Sampler*
    Čučnik, Pepelnik, Podlogar,
    Šalamun, Škrjanec

23 *The Life and Opinions of
    DJ Spinoza*
    Eugene Ostashevsky

24 *What Do You Want*
    Marina Temkina

25 *Parrot on a Motorcycle*
    Vítězslav Nezval

26 *Look Back, Look Ahead*
    Srečko Kosovel

27 *Try a Little Time Travel*
    Natalie Lyalin

28 *Thirty-Five New Pages*
    Lev Rubinstein

29 *On the Tracks of Wild Game*
    Tomaž Šalamun

30 *It's No Good*
    Kirill Medvedev

31 *I Live I See*
    Vsevolod Nekrasov

32 *A Science Not for The Earth*
    Yevgeny Baratynsky

33 *The Compleat Catalogue of
    Comedic Novelties*
    Lev Rubinstein

34 *Blood Makes Me Faint
    But I Go for It*
    Natalie Lyalin

35 *Morse, My Deaf Friend*
    Miloš Djurdjević

36 *What We Saw from
    This Mountain*
    Vladimir Aristov

37 *Hit Parade: The Orbita Group*
    Kevin Platt, ed.

38 *Written in the Dark: Five Poets
    in the Siege of Leningrad*
    Polina Barskova, ed.

39 *Elementary Poetry*
    Andrei Monastyrski

40 *Kholin 66: Diaries and Poems*
    Igor Kholin

41 *Letter to the Amazon*
    Marina Tsvetaeva

42 *Moss & Silver*
    Jure Detela

43 *Gestures*
    Artis Ostups

44 *Alphabet for the Entrants*
    Vasilisk Gnedov

45 *Soviet Texts*
    Dmitri Alexandrovich Prigov

46 *Life In Space*
    Galina Rymbu

47 *Air Raid*
    Polina Barskova

48 *New Hull*
    Mikhail Kuzmin

49 *[Selected Poems]*
    Dmitri Kuzmin